99 Ideas and Activities for Teaching English Learners with the SIOP® Model

MaryEllen Vogt

California State University, Long Beach

Jana Echevarría

California State University, Long Beach

PEARSON

Boston   New York   San Francisco
Mexico City   Montreal   Toronto   London   Madrid   Munich   Paris
Hong Kong   Singapore   Tokyo   Cape Town   Sydney

Executive Editor: Aurora Martínez Ramos
Editorial Assistant: Lynda Giles
Marketing Manager: Danae April
Production Editor: Gregory Erb
Editorial Production Service: Nesbitt Graphics, Inc.
Composition Buyer: Linda Cox
Manufacturing Buyer: Linda Morris
Electronic Composition: Nesbitt Graphics, Inc.
Interior Design: Nesbitt Graphics, Inc.
Cover Designer: Kristina Mose-Libon

For related titles and support materials, visit our online catalog at www.ablongman.com.

28   16

contents

Over the past decade, we have worked with thousands of teachers and administrators throughout the United States and several other countries as they have implemented the SIOP® Model. The term SIOP® (pronounced *sigh-op*), the acronym for the Sheltered Instruction Observation Protocol, has become widely known as an empirically validated approach for implementing effective sheltered content instruction for students who are acquiring English as a second (or multiple) language. The SIOP® Model, derived from the SIOP® observation protocol, includes eight instructional components and thirty features that, when used in combination consistently and systematically, have been found to improve English learners' academic achievement (Echevarria, Short, & Powers, 2006; Echevarria, Vogt, & Short, 2008).

This book responds to frequent requests from elementary and secondary teachers for additional teaching ideas, activities, and approaches that can be used to effectively implement the SIOP® Model. The ideas and activities, as well as other information within this book, are grouped within each of the eight SIOP® components.

Criteria for Selecting the Ideas and Activities

As you look through this book, you will undoubtedly recognize some familiar ideas and activities; we hope you will also find new approaches and support for making the content you teach more comprehensible for English learners (and other students). These ideas and activities were selected according to the following criteria:

- They focus on providing English learners with practice and application of key content and language concepts;
- They promote students' interactions with each other and with the teacher;
- They provide opportunities for students to use English while reading, writing, listening, and speaking;
- They can be implemented with ease for nearly any subject area or grade level;
- They provide information for the teacher to use for review and assessment of content and language objectives.

The SIOP® Model serves as an instructional framework for sheltered instruction that values effective, research-based, and time-honored teaching practices. Many of the cooperative learning and other techniques you already use are appropriate to include in SIOP® lessons. These new ideas and activities have been recommended by experienced SIOP® teachers and will add to your repertoire, further enhancing your instruction and your students' learning.

About This Book

If you are currently teaching or working with teachers, it is important to remember that *activities are not the end*; they are the means to the end. The end, of course, is mastery by all students of content objectives, language objectives, and district/state content standards. Although some teachers just want "use-tomorrow" activities for activities' sake, as fellow teachers, coaches, and supervisors, we all have a responsibility to help these teachers learn to use a variety of instructional techniques in a purposeful, thoughtful, and careful manner to maximize student achievement.

Content and Language Objectives

It is our expectation that anyone who is reading this book has already read the core text, *Making Content Comprehensible for English Learners: The SIOP® Model (3rd Ed.,* Echevarria, Vogt, & Short, 2008). This book is essential for a thorough understanding of the SIOP® Model, which includes the need for explicit content and language objectives for each and every sheltered content lesson. If you have participated in SIOP® training, you know the critical importance of including content and language objectives that are explicitly stated, shared in writing, and presented orally to students.

Our research confirms that content and language objectives must guide the selection of appropriate and meaningful activities; activities that provide English learners with varied opportunities to practice and apply content knowledge at the same time ELs are developing English proficiency. The lesson-level content and language objectives must be observable (the teacher or observer should be able to see students actively working to meet an objective), and measurable (the teacher or observer should be able to determine whether students are making progress toward or have met each objective).

Learning behaviors, therefore, must be stated very specifically, such as: "Students will be able to identify three reasons why. . ."; "Students will be able to compare and contrast two perspectives related to. . ."; "Students will be able to classify into three groups the following. . ." These objectives could also be stated as "I can. . ." statements to better facilitate student understandings: "I can identify three reasons why. . ."; "I can compare and contrast two perspectives related to. . ."; or "I can classify into three groups the following. . ."

Note that on these somewhat generic objectives, we left off a specific subject area or topic. For a given lesson, the topic must be included: "The student will be able to (or "I can") compare and contrast the perspectives of Civil War Generals Ulysses S. Grant and Robert E. Lee regarding strategies for winning the war in 1863." Or: "I can compare and contrast a square and a rectangle." Note that these sample objectives are observable and measurable by the teacher.

Content and language objectives are included as examples for nearly all of the ideas and activities in this book. Many are stated somewhat generically with the expectation that you will insert the topic/subject area you are teaching just as we did above. On these objectives you will see the parenthetical words, "a topic." For example, with the Anticipation/Reaction Guide (p. 82) in the Strategies section, you find the following content objective: "Students will be able to agree or disagree about Anticipation statements written about (a topic)." If the subject you are teaching is social studies/current events, and the topic is capital punishment, your content objective for the students might read: "I can agree or disagree with Anticipation statements about capital punishment." A language objective might be: "I can orally or in writing justify my reasoning for agreeing or disagreeing with Anticipation statements about capital punishment."

For example, when teaching second graders a unit on Our Community in social studies, write five Anticipation statements about what children can do to make their communities a better place. A content objective might be: Students will be able to agree or disagree with statements about their roles in their community and give reasons for their positions.

A language objective might be: Students will be able to complete sentences about their community and share them orally with their partner using one of the following sentence stems:

"I agree with this statement because. . ."

"I disagree with this statement because. . ."

- For younger children (K-2), the stems might be:

"I say yes because. . ."

"I say no because. . ."

Our purpose in providing generic objectives is to help you learn how to frame objectives for your English learners. Remember that all lesson objectives, both content and language, must be generated from actual content; your district and/or state standards will most likely serve as your guide. Never introduce generic objectives to students such as, "The students will use a Venn diagram," or "The students will complete a graphic organizer." The objectives do not spring from the activity; they are generated by the key content and language concepts being taught. State specifically the learning behaviors you plan to elicit (e.g., explain, diagram, discuss, predict, summarize, draw, list, etc.). Include the specific content and language concepts you are teaching and reinforcing.

Lesson Plans

At the end of each chapter for six of the SIOP® components (Building Background, Comprehensible Input, Strategies, Interaction, Practice/Application, Review/Assessment) you will find two comprehensive lesson plans, one written at the elementary and one at the secondary level. These are complete lessons that illustrate how you might use an idea or activity in the respective component to implement the features of the SIOP® Model. Despite the fact that we have included instructional ideas and activities here component by component, in reality the SIOP® Model integrates the components (and thus the features) throughout a lesson. Accomplished SIOP® teachers don't plan a lesson one component at a time; their lessons demonstrate the overlap, interrelatedness, and integration among the SIOP® components.

For example, an activity such as The Insert Method (p. 33) might activate prior knowledge and build students' backgrounds, but it can also make content comprehensible by teaching learning strategies (such as monitoring comprehension), promoting interaction between partners, and providing for practice and application of the key content and language concepts. During a lesson with The Insert Method, teachers continually review and assess students' understanding. Although an idea or activity "resides" within one or two components in this book, in reality these activities support and reinforce student learning of key content and language concepts across the components and features of the SIOP® Model, from lesson to lesson. This important point is illustrated by each of the lesson plans at the end of the chapters.

Note how the lesson plans are derived from the content and lesson objectives. Within each lesson plan, the content and language objectives are numbered (such as 1, 2, etc.). Follow across the page (left to right) and you will find meaningful activities that are also numbered (1.1, 2.1). The activities were specifically selected so that students can practice and apply the key content and language concepts described in the objectives. You will also see that the teachers assessment of student learning corresponds to the numbers of the lesson's content and language objectives. The lesson plans all incorporate ideas and activities from this book, and they were created to illustrate how to promote student attainment of the respective content and language objectives.

Finally, the lesson plans span a variety of grade levels to encourage the use of these ideas and activities across the pre-K-12 continuum. Most of the activities can be used at any grade level, but several are most effective in the lower or upper grades and these have been identified accordingly.

Acknowledgements

We have made every attempt to identity the originators of the ideas and activities that are included in this publication; we thank them for their creative, effective approaches to teaching and learning. If you know of anyone that we did not include, please let us know.

We enthusiastically acknowledge our reviewers, whose insights, understanding of the SIOP® Model, helpful suggestions, and additional ideas and activities were greatly appreciated. They include: Julia S. Austin, University of Alabama, Birmingham; Gwendelyn Silva, California State University, Fullerton; Karen Fichter, Zebulon GT Magnet Middle School; Carla Dudley, Oak Mountain Intermediate School.

We are grateful to five expert SIOP® teachers for their help with this book: Angie Medina, who shared many ideas that she and her colleagues in the Long Beach Unified School District have used with their English learners; Nicole Teyechea, a SIOP® Institute National Faculty member who created, with Melissa Castillo, the effective lesson plan format; Kendra Moreno, for her help with ideas and lesson planning; Sarah Russell, a SIOP® National Faculty member and superb ESL teacher, and Melissa Castillo, also a member of the SIOP® Institute National Faculty, for her creative and well-written lesson plans, additional teaching ideas and activities, and expertise in teaching with the SIOP® Model. We have learned a great deal from these extraordinary educators about teaching and learning with the SIOP® Model.

Finally, we express our thanks to our SIOP® colleague and friend, Deborah Short, and to our families who lovingly (and with great patience) support our work.

mev   je

a guide to using this book

The name of the activity

Which of the eight components the activity supports

How the activity supports the SIOP® Model

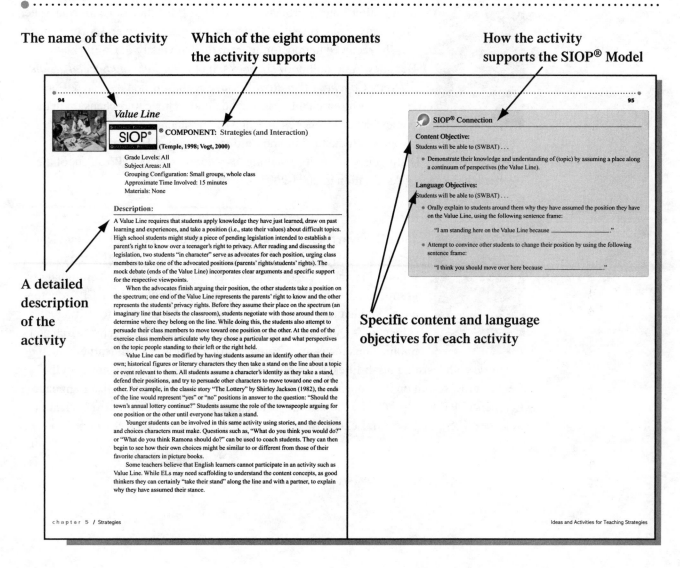

94

Value Line

SIOP® **COMPONENT:** Strategies (and Interaction)
(Temple, 1998; Vogt, 2000)

Grade Levels: All
Subject Areas: All
Grouping Configuration: Small groups, whole class
Approximate Time Involved: 15 minutes
Materials: None

Description:

A Value Line requires that students apply knowledge they have just learned, draw on past learning and experiences, and take a position (i.e., state their values) about difficult topics. High school students might study a piece of pending legislation intended to establish a parent's right to know over a teenager's right to privacy. After reading and discussing the legislation, two students "in character" serve as advocates for each position, urging class members to take one of the advocated positions (parents' rights/students' rights). The mock debate (ends of the Value Line) incorporates clear arguments and specific support for the respective viewpoints.

When the advocates finish arguing their position, the other students take a position on the spectrum; one end of the Value Line represents the parents' right to know and the other represents the students' privacy rights. Before they assume their place on the spectrum (an imaginary line that bisects the classroom), students negotiate with those around them to determine where they belong on the line. While doing this, the students also attempt to persuade their class members to move toward one position or the other. At the end of the exercise class members articulate why they chose a particular spot and what perspectives on the topic people standing to their left or the right held.

Value Line can be modified by having students assume an identify other than their own; historical figures or literary characters they then take a stand on the line about a topic or event relevant to them. All students assume a character's identity as they take a stand, defend their positions, and try to persuade other characters to move toward one end or the other. For example, in the classic story "The Lottery" by Shirley Jackson (1982), the ends of the line would represent "yes" or "no" positions in answer to the question: "Should the town's annual lottery continue?" Students assume the role of the townspeople arguing for one position or the other until everyone has taken a stand.

Younger students can be involved in this same activity using stories, and the decisions and choices characters must make. Questions such as, "What do you think you would do?" or "What do you think Ramona should do?" can be used to coach students. They can then begin to see how their own choices might be similar to or different from those of their favorite characters in picture books.

Some teachers believe that English learners cannot participate in an activity such as Value Line. While ELs may need scaffolding to understand the content concepts, as good thinkers they can certainly "take their stand" along the line and with a partner, to explain why they have assumed their stance.

95

🔍 SIOP® Connection

Content Objective:
Students will be able to (SWBAT) . . .

• Demonstrate their knowledge and understanding of (topic) by assuming a place along a continuum of perspectives (the Value Line).

Language Objectives:
Students will be able to (SWBAT) . . .

• Orally explain to students around them why they have assumed the position they have on the Value Line, using the following sentence frame:

"I am standing here on the Value Line because _____."

• Attempt to convince other students to change their position by using the following sentence frame:

"I think you should move over here because _____."

A detailed description of the activity

Specific content and language objectives for each activity

About the Authors

MaryEllen Vogt is Professor Emerita of Education at California State University, Long Beach. A former reading specialist and special educator, she received her doctorate from the University of California, Berkeley. A co-author of six books, including *Reading Specialists and Literacy Coaches in the Real World,* Second Edition, (Allyn & Bacon, 2007), her research interests include improving comprehension in the content areas, teacher change and development, and content literacy for English learners. Dr. Vogt was inducted into the California Reading Hall of Fame and received CSULB's Distinguished Faculty Teaching Award. She served as President of the International Reading Association in 2004-2005.

Jana Echevarria is a Professor of Education at California State University, Long Beach. She has taught in elementary, middle and high schools in general education, special education, ESL and bilingual programs. She has lived in Taiwan, Spain and Mexico. Her UCLA doctorate earned her an award from the National Association for Bilingual Education's Outstanding Dissertations Competition. Her research and publications focus on effective instruction for English learners, including those with learning disabilities. Currently, she is Co-Principal Investigator with the Center for Research on the Educational Achievement and Teaching of English Language Learners (CREATE) funded by the U.S. Department of Education, Institute of Education Sciences (IES). In 2005, Dr. Echevarria was selected as Outstanding Professor at CSULB.

chapter 1

Overview of the SIOP® Model

In the mid-1990's increasing numbers of English learners (ELs) were entering public schools in the United States. Educators, particularly ESL (English as a Second Language) and bilingual teachers, began receiving professional development in how to teach recently arrived immigrant students whose home language was not English. The techniques and methods that were shared during in-services, workshops, and university classes consisted primarily of a range of ESL instructional strategies, and sheltered instruction, an approach that extends the time students have for receiving English language support while they learn content subjects. The ultimate goal of sheltered instruction is to provide access for ELs to grade-level content standards and concepts while they continue to improve their English language proficiency. Generally, sheltered content classes (such as math, science, and social studies) have included English learners with varying levels of English proficiency, and in some cases, a mix of both native English speakers and ELs. In sheltered classes, the language of instruction is English.[1]

In a few states (such as California), legislation was enacted that required teachers to receive professional development in how to teach English learners. However, when we (Jana and MaryEllen on the west coast, and Deborah Short on the east coast) visited classrooms and observed subject area lessons taught by these newly prepared teachers, we did not see many who were implementing effective sheltered lessons for English learners. After discussions among ourselves and with colleagues across the country, we realized that even though there were instructional techniques recommended in the ESL literature, there was little agreement about what effective sheltered instruction was and how it should "look" during lessons. Definitions and descriptions varied widely across the country, with most including a list of activities and techniques, few of which had been empirically validated with English learners. To further compound the problem, most school administrators were not receiving professional development in the unique learning and language needs of ELs. They were therefore unable to provide their teachers with instructional assistance about the needs of English learners after lesson observations and during conferences.

In 1995 we began the process of creating an observation protocol that could be used by researchers, administrators, university supervisors, coaches, and teachers. Our goal was to operationalize sheltered instruction so that educators would have a common language to use when discussing appropriate content instruction for ELs. We were convinced that English learners do not have the luxury of waiting to learn content until they have mastered English. Instead, they must be able to develop English language proficiency and content knowledge concurrently. All teachers who have ELs in their classrooms must know how to implement effective sheltered instruction consistently and systematically. Therefore, a common definition and instructional framework for this important instructional approach was needed.

Using research findings on ESL/bilingual methods, articles on best practice, and our own experiences as teachers (elementary, middle, and high school; regular education, ESL/bilingual, special education, and language/literacy specialization), we began to create what ultimately became the Sheltered Instruction Observation Protocol or SIOP® (pronounced *sigh-op*). Throughout the developmental process (which occurred over five-years), we collaborated closely with teachers who helped shape our thinking, field-tested the SIOP® in their own classrooms, implemented the SIOP® components with their students, and eventually became project teachers for a federally funded grant through the Center for Research on Education, Diversity, and Excellence (CREDE) (see Echevarria, Vogt, & Short, 2008 for detailed information about the research project and findings). The teacher-researcher collaboration greatly enhanced the SIOP® as it evolved through 22 iterations to its present form.

As you review the eight components and thirty features of the SIOP® Model, many, if not most, will be familiar to you. Our original task was to take what we know to be effective instructional techniques (such as increasing wait-time after questioning), and determine if they positively impact the student achievement of ELs when used consistently and

---

[1]Note that as the SIOP® Model is implemented outside of the U.S., the language of instruction may vary. Currently, the Model is being implemented in all 50 states, the U.S. territories, and several other countries.

in combination. At the conclusion of the research study, the English learners in the class-rooms of teachers who fully implemented the 30 SIOP® features outperformed (on a standardized measure) those ELs in classrooms where teachers had received professional development in sheltered instruction, but not specifically in the SIOP® Model (see Echevarria, Short, & Powers, 2006).

The components and a description of the features of the SIOP® Model follow (see Appendix A for the complete Sheltered Instruction Observation Protocol):

1. *Preparation:* Teachers plan lessons carefully, paying particular attention to language and content objectives, appropriate content concepts, the use of supplemental materials, adaptation of content, and meaningful activities.

2. *Building Background:* Teachers make explicit links to their students' background experiences and knowledge, and past learning, and teach and emphasize key vocabulary.

3. *Comprehensible Input:* Teachers use a variety of techniques to make instruction understandable, including speech appropriate to students' English proficiency, clear academic tasks, modeling, and the use of visuals, hands-on activities, demonstrations, gestures, and body language.

4. *Strategies:* Teachers provide students with instruction in and practice with a variety of learning strategies, scaffolding their teaching with techniques such as think-alouds, and they promote higher-order thinking through a variety of question types and levels.

5. *Interaction:* Teachers provide students with frequent opportunities for interaction and discussion, group students to support content and language objectives, provide sufficient wait-time for student responses, and appropriately clarify concepts in the student's first language, if possible and necessary.

6. *Practice and Application:* Teachers provide hands-on materials and/or manipulatives, and include activities for students to apply their content and language knowledge through all language skills (reading, writing, listening, and speaking).

7. *Lesson Delivery:* Teachers implement lessons that clearly support content and language objectives with appropriate pacing, while students are engaged 90–100 percent of the instructional period.

8. *Review and Assessment:* Teachers provide a comprehensive review of key vocabulary and concepts, regularly give specific, academic feedback to students, and conduct assessment of student comprehension and learning throughout the lesson.

What began as an observation protocol has now evolved into an empirically validated model of instruction for English learners, where the focus is on the concurrent teaching and learning of both language and content. While the SIOP® Model was originally substantiated with middle school students, it is now being implemented in pre-K-12 throughout the U.S. Our research has shown that given sustained professional development (from 1–3 years), teachers can learn to implement the 30 features consistently and systematically from lesson to lesson. Current longitudinal research studies are investigating the efficacy of the SIOP® Model with varied student populations.

If you are new to the SIOP® Model, it is *very* important that you read carefully the core text, *Making Content Comprehensible for English Learners: The SIOP® Model, Third*

Edition. (Echevarria, Vogt, & Short, 2008). This book, *99 Ideas and Activities for Teaching English Learners with the SIOP® Model,* is intended to be a companion to the original text, not a replacement for it. As you learn more about the SIOP® Model, you will see that it involves complex teaching practices that must be used in combination daily. Therefore, our recommendation is that teachers who are learning the SIOP® Model go slowly—perhaps implementing one component a month or quarter. It is not unusual for a school that has adopted the SIOP® Model to take two or three years for full implementation. The observation protocol (see Appendix A) is at the heart of the SIOP® Model. Its use as a lesson planning guide, an observation (*not* evaluation) instrument, and as the focus of conferences and discussion is critical to the success of SIOP® implementation.

chapter 2

Preparation

Overview of Preparation Component

As new teachers, one of the most important things we learned was to carefully prepare each lesson, and in the early days, lesson plans were often several pages long. As we became more experienced the planning process was quicker and easier . . . and at some point, our lesson plan fit neatly into a 4 × 4 inch box in a lesson planning book! Working over the years with SIOP® teachers, we have rediscovered the value of thoughtful, detailed lesson planning.

For teachers new to the SIOP® Model, the lesson planning process may resemble those early experiences we had as new teachers: struggling to write "behavioral objectives." Perhaps you never learned to write specific lesson objectives and have relied on district and/or state content standards as a guide. Within the SIOP® Model, both standards and lesson-specific objectives are of critical importance.

Progress Report
- Report Card Grades
- Teacher Training
- Stipends
- Grants
- Community Partners

Content objectives are created from district and state content standards, but rather than being global, as some standards are, they are specific to the lesson content being taught. Language objectives are intended to guide lesson design and implementation so that English learners develop English proficiency and vocabulary knowledge concurrently with subject matter understandings.

As SIOP® teachers begin to think about the importance of including content and language objectives for each and every lesson, their selection of instructional materials, techniques, and activities is more deliberate and purposeful. It becomes evident that the texts that are appropriate for many native English speakers may not be suitable for students acquiring English—the content and text must be adapted for ELs' comprehensibility and accessibility. Similarly, "dumbing down" the content concepts taught to English learners, a practice all-too-common for many years—can no longer be accepted. All students, regardless of home language, must have access to appropriate grade-level content concepts and vocabulary. Teachers must use whatever they can, modeling, realia, photographs, demonstrations, illustrations, and so forth, to help ELs develop content knowledge while they're learning English. These supplemental materials must be considered during the lesson planning process, along with relevant and meaningful activities for practicing and applying content and language knowledge. Not surprisingly, lesson planning may require more thought, time, and attention in the early stages of implementing the SIOP® Model.

The Preparation component includes these features:

1. Content objectives clearly defined for students.

2. Language objectives clearly defined for students.

3. Content concepts appropriate for age and educational background level of students.

4. Supplementary materials used to a high degree, making the lesson clear and meaningful (e.g., computer programs, graphs, models, visuals).

5. Adaptation of content (e.g., text, assignment) to all levels of student proficiency.

6. Meaningful activities that integrate lesson concepts (e.g., interviews, letter writing, simulations, models) with language practice opportunities for reading, writing, listening, and/or speaking.

Ideas and Activities for Enhancing Lesson Preparation

Teacher Collaboration Using the SIOP® Protocol

COMPONENT: Preparation

Grade Levels: All
Subject Levels: All
Grouping Configurations: None (teacher planning)
Approximate Time Involved: 30 minutes while planning lesson/unit
Materials: The SIOP® Protocol

Description:

Once teachers become comfortable with the SIOP® protocol, professional development begins by assessing their own instruction based on the protocol's rating scale. It is important, however, for teachers to realize that the SIOP® protocol is not meant for teacher *evaluation,* but rather as a tool to measure the effectiveness of a sheltered instruction lesson.

Teachers working in schools in which the SIOP® Model is being implemented have found it helpful to collaborate with fellow teachers when planning lessons. Likewise, these teachers, usually at the same grade level, can reflect on lessons together checking their fidelity to the SIOP® Model.

For example, a grade level team meets to plan a lesson using the SIOP® protocol as a checklist to make certain all of the components and features are well represented in the lesson. Next, the teachers deliver the lesson to their own students. The teachers then meet to discuss the success and challenges of using the SIOP® protocol. This accomplishes several objectives:

- Teachers can reflect upon their instruction for strengths and areas that need improvement while examining the SIOP® protocol;
- Teachers become familiar with the SIOP® Model's eight components and 30 features and articulate the rationale for implementing a particular feature;
- Teachers collaborate with colleagues to improve instruction for the English learners by discussing the features of an effective sheltered instruction lesson;
- Teachers engage in an assessment of a lesson's effectiveness, rather than an evaluation of a teacher; this is best accomplished when teachers observe each other's teaching and use of the SIOP® protocol, either through a "live" observation or by watching a videotaped lesson;
- Teachers set individual goals for improved implementation of specific features of the SIOP® Model; growth is measured in reflective steps not leaps.

SIOP® Connection

This particular Preparation idea does not lend itself to specific content or language objectives for students.

Differentiated Instruction

COMPONENT: Preparation

Grade Levels: All

Subject Areas: All

Grouping Configurations: Not Applicable

Approximate Time Involved: 30 minutes while planning lesson or unit

Materials: Carefully written content and language objectives for particular lessons

Description:

Students come to school with a variety of backgrounds, abilities, learning styles, and English proficiency levels. In order to meet the needs of all students, differentiated instruction is necessary. The SIOP® Model provides a framework for planning and delivering effective sheltered instruction, and can also serve as a guide for developing differentiated lessons. The following questions focus on the six Preparation features:

1. *Clearly defined content objectives:*
   "How will I meet the needs of all learners so that they can achieve grade level standards?"

   Once teachers have determined students' academic and language proficiency levels, they can begin designing lessons that target those needs. Differentiated instruction involves all students working toward the same objectives, but in different ways, in different grouping configurations, and perhaps with different texts and instructional materials. Clearly written and stated content objectives are needed to provide a road-map for both students and teachers, regardless of group assignment or instructional materials. During and at the end of each lesson, when the content objectives are assessed, teachers can determine who has met them and who has not— further appropriate differentiated instruction can then be provided as needed.

2. *Clearly defined language objectives:*
   "How will I plan for multilevel responses according to students' English proficiency levels?"

   It is crucial that teachers know their students well so that opportunities can be provided for them to practice English in a comfortable, but challenging, classroom environment. Teachers must maintain high, yet reasonable expectations for student output based on the lesson's content and language objectives. For example, some students may be able to demonstrate their understandings through pantomime or illustration, while others can respond to questions with complete sentences and/or written paragraphs. To make determinations about students' comprehension, you must know both what they can understand (receptive: such as reading and listening) and what they can produce (expressive: such as writing and speaking).

   If you don't know a student's English proficiency level, it is imperative that you request that information from your school or district's ESL teacher coordinator. If there is not an ESL specialist in your school or district, it is important that you advocate for such a position. Estimating a child's English proficiency is not sufficient when several respected assessments that provide this information are available. ELs deserve this type of assessment and educational support—advocate strongly for it.

As with content objectives, language objectives that are clearly stated provide a road-map for developing English language proficiency for students with diverse needs.

3. *Appropriate content concepts for students' age and background:*
"How do I plan appropriate grade-level instruction for my English learners if they do not have the requisite knowledge to understand what is being taught?"

Effective SIOP® teachers know that it is inappropriate to ignore grade-level content standards when teaching English learners. But many immigrant students lack specific content knowledge due to interrupted or nonexistent schooling experiences in their home countries, or to mismatches in the EL's school experiences and the grade-level expectations of their new schools. Other students arrive in the U.S. with comprehensive schooling experiences in their home country, so their primary goal is to learn English and transfer what they know to their new classroom.

Therefore, within the SIOP® Model, teachers learn to teach grade-level standards and objectives, while adapting and adjusting instruction for students' particular needs. Adaptations to texts and content are appropriate as long as expectations for grade-level content mastery for all students remain high. It may take English learners longer to reach mastery, but with appropriate differentiated instruction, the expectation is that they will do so.

4. *Supplementary materials used to a high degree:*
"How can I clarify concepts for struggling students? How can I present concepts in a way that is relevant and meaningful?"

Differentiated instruction allows students to demonstrate new knowledge in a variety of ways. English learners may need additional, or different, opportunities to use supplementary materials. A variety of learning styles will likely be represented in one classroom, making it imperative that a range of materials is available. Hands-on manipulatives, illustrations, graphic organizers, adapted texts, taped texts, photographs, and electronic resources are examples of the types of supplemental materials that can be used to enhance student understanding.

5. *Adaptation of content to all levels of student proficiency:*
"How do I make the content material accessible for all students?"

One of the challenges SIOP® teachers face is the number of English proficiency levels represented in one classroom. This becomes particularly difficult in regard to grade level texts. While it may not be necessary to adapt the content for all students, ELs benefit from partially completed graphic organizers, partially filled-in outlines, highlighted texts (e.g., topic sentences, key vocabulary, and key concepts), marginal notes, and rewritten, adapted text. Many publishers include adapted texts and summaries with their grade-level text books for this purpose; these make content learning much more accessible for English learners. Remember that content standards should not be watered down in adapted materials.

6. *Meaningful activities that integrate lesson concepts:*
"How will I organize my classroom for a variety of meaningful activities to occur at once?"

Differentiating instruction means preparing for a variety of grouping configurations and activities to occur at one time. Students may be working independently, in cooperative groups or with the teacher, based on assessed needs. Some students may require more modeling and examples, others will be ready to strike out on their own.

Teachers need to ensure that while students are involved with activities that allow for language practice, content standards are also supported: Students may practice in different ways but are all learning the same content information.

> ### SIOP® Connection
>
> These ideas related to the Preparation component do not lend themselves to specific content or language objectives for students.

Enlarged, Adapted Text

Grade Levels: 3–12
Subject Areas: All
Grouping Configurations: Individual, partners, small groups, whole class
Approximate Time Involved: Depends on length of text
Materials: Any context text that can be enlarged through re-typing or photocopying

Description:

Textbooks can often be intimidating and overwhelming for English learners. Many include small size font in expository text, distracting pictures, enlarged, colorful captions with comments along the side. Therefore, many students don't know where to focus their attention. Does the boxed text include the most important information, or is it merely interesting and entertaining? Where is the essential information on the page? You can help English learners (and struggling students) with these questions by providing them with enlarged font and adapted text. By doing so, you are providing your students with clues about where to find information and a clear focus on what they need to learn.

This is a simple process:

1. Type text with an enlarged font (approximately 300 words).
2. Focus on only 3–5 bolded vocabulary words (a textbook might have 15, which is too many).
3. Encourage students to use highlighters to mark words they recognize.
4. Show students how to highlight and/or underline important concepts prior to attempting to read the text.
5. Show younger students and beginning English speakers how to draw pictures on the text's page to reflect vocabulary and conceptual understandings. These can serve as reminders as well as mnemonics for remembering key information.

Enlarged, adapted text lowers anxiety for both new readers and students who are acquiring English proficiency. Teachers of heterogeneous classes, that include both English learners and native English speakers, sometimes ask if enlarged, adapted text will point out students with special needs. Our response is that the kids already know who these students are—it is your job as the teacher to provide instructional assistance however you can. It is appropriate for you to have conversations with your students so they understand that not all students will be working with the same instructional materials.

SIOP® Connection

Content Objectives:

Students will be able to (SWBAT) . . .

- Identify, with a highlighter, (a key concept) from each paragraph about (a topic) in enlarged, adapted text.

(continued)

SIOP® Connection *(continued)*

- Identify with a highlighter and define three vocabulary words (specify) from the enlarged, adapted text.

Language Objective:

Students will be able to (SWBAT) . . .

- Orally paraphrase, with a partner, the three key concepts about (the topic) after reading the enlarged, adapted text.

Alternate Materials

SIOP® **COMPONENT:** Preparation

Grade Levels: All
Subject Areas: All
Grouping Configuration: Individual, partners, small group, whole class
Materials: An assortment of stimulating "props" for making the content being taught more comprehensible.

Description:

Use as many materials as needed to make content comprehensible to students. The more variation, the better you will be able to connect with different students' learning styles and background experiences. For example:

1. Use pictures from books, magazines, travel brochures, and photographs.
2. Don't settle for black line masters of maps. Find authentic, real maps.
3. Give pictorial support by using videos or snippets of videos.
4. Bring in experts and people from the community to share personal collections and experiences.
5. Use realia (real objects) when possible. For example, when students are studying rocks, have them find rocks around the school or their homes to bring to class.
6. When students are literate in their primary language, occasionally let them read about the curriculam content in their L1 (student's native language) if possible.
7. Have students draw pictures of their own experiences to make connections to the content. Encourage them to use these pictures to share and teach others in the class. In a high school history class, for example, ELs (and other students, if appropriate) keep key vocabulary words and definitions on index cards they illustrate with a quick sketch, which serves as an effective mnemonic for remembering the words.
8. Find (on the Internet) and use clip art that goes with a unit to illustrate key concepts and vocabulary.
9. Use literature, poetry, and music to reinforce key points about content concepts.
10. Field trips and excursions help students create first hand knowledge about a subject.
11. When possible, use hands-on activities such as classifying, sorting, posting, Gallery Walks, and so forth, to reinforce learning.
12. Find and/or create timelines that display chronological events.
13. Bring in food to display content concepts. For example, make pancakes with added ingredients to show the metamorphic processes of melting, changing size, shape, and color.
14. Let students create their own classroom materials. For example, bring in Play Doh to illustrate the layers of the earth's surface.

15. Graphic organizers can help students visually organize and remember new information. Once information has been organized on a graphic organizer, simply seeing the visual cue will help students recall information. For beginning English speakers, provide scaffolding with a partially completed graphic organizer by including the headings and/or a few details.

SIOP® Connection

The following example shows how a teacher might use Cuisinaire rods and symbol cards to teach, reinforce, and practice simple equations.

Content Objectives:

Students will be able to (SWBAT) . . .

- Demonstrate their understanding of "greater than," "less than," and "equals" by placing Cuisinaire rods in an equation using the symbol cards >, <, and = (see Figure 2.1).
- Compute simple numerical equations using the symbols > and <.

Language Objective:

Students will be able to (SWBAT) . . .

- Read and write equations with number words and the terms "greater than," "less than," and "equals."

FIGURE 2.1 *Alternate Materials*

Success through Scaffolding

COMPONENT: Preparation

Grade Levels: 2–12
Subject Levels: All
Grouping Configurations: None (teacher planning)
Materials: None (teacher planning)

Description:

We believe that scaffolding student learning is critically important for student achievement, as evidenced by the separate scaffolding feature found in the Strategies component. The purpose of Success through Scaffolding, as suggested here, is to make our scaffolding efforts transparent to students as they move from dependence on the teacher to independence.

The first steps of teaching a new concept should be explicit, followed by careful modeling. As instruction becomes more self-guided and grouping configurations are in place, students become more dependent on one another, decreasing their dependence on the teacher. As students gain confidence and experience, more supports are removed and students are able to work independently with a particular strategy and content concept. During planning, it is important to remember that this process does not take place in one lesson, but rather through a sequence of lessons in which the students experience Success through Scaffolding as they move towards independence.

Generally, teachers teach lessons without explaining to students how the sequence of activities is designed to prepare them for independence. English learners, however, benefit from knowing how to identify what is helpful to them, how to ask for assistance, and how to self-assess the degree to which they are learning a new process or concept. With Success through Scaffolding, the teacher consciously makes scaffolding techniques transparent, such as through modeling, demonstration, repetition, varied grouping arrangements, and paraphrasing. These scaffolding techniques are explained and discussed with EL students so they learn how to use them to their advantage.

SIOP® Connection

These objectives exemplify how teachers may help older students take responsibility for their own learning by articulating when they need additional assistance and support, and when they are able to work independently.

Content Objectives:

Students will be able to (SWBAT) . . .

- Identify the varying levels of support they receive in the classroom.
- Identify when the teacher is modeling a task or an assignment.

(continued)

SIOP® Connection *(continued)*

- Identify when and why group support with other students is helpful and appropriate.
- Identify when and why working independently to demonstrate individual thought and understanding is beneficial.

Language Objectives:

Students will be able to (SWBAT) . . .

- Articulate when they need assistance.
- Use four key phrases to solicit support from the teacher or from another student:

    "I don't understand."
    "Would you please explain that to me?"
    "Would you please model that for me?"
    "Would you please demonstrate that for me?"

Task Analysis or Backwards Planning

COMPONENT: Preparation

Grade Levels: All*
Subject Levels: All
Grouping Configuration: None (teacher planning)
Approximate Time Involved: 5–20 minutes during lesson preparation
Materials: Lesson plans and content/language objectives

Description:

The purpose of Task Analysis (or Backwards Planning) is to ensure that instruction leads to student success on the final assessment of a lesson's content and language objectives. During lesson planning, the teacher determines how the content and language objectives will be assessed. When the assessment is predetermined, a quick pretest can then be used to assess prior knowledge about the content concepts. A predetermined assessment keeps the instruction focused on the lesson objectives and creates an environment for success.

It is important for teachers to plan backward from the final assessment, thinking about what students need to know and be able to do in order to be successful on the assessment of content and language objectives. If students are unable to understand and/or complete a task, the teacher should step back, reteach, and explain the concept in a different way before moving on. Too often, teachers do not realize until the final assessment that some students have been lost throughout the lesson. Task Analysis can prevent this from happening.

If, at the beginning of a lesson, the teacher explains how students will be assessed, then when the content and language objectives are presented, students will better understand how instruction and tasks correlate with the eventual assessment.

SIOP® Connection

Task Analysis does not lend itself to specific content or language objectives for students.

---

*While Task Analysis is important for all grade levels, older students (grades 3–12) will benefit most from a careful explanation of how lessons are planned and taught.

SIOP® Planning Flow Chart

COMPONENT: Preparation

(Adapted from Long Beach Unified School District)

Grade Levels: All
Subject Levels: All
Grouping Configuration: None (teacher planning)
Approximate Time Involved: 30 minutes to one hour during unit preparation
Materials: SIOP® Planning Flow Chart (see Figure 2.2)

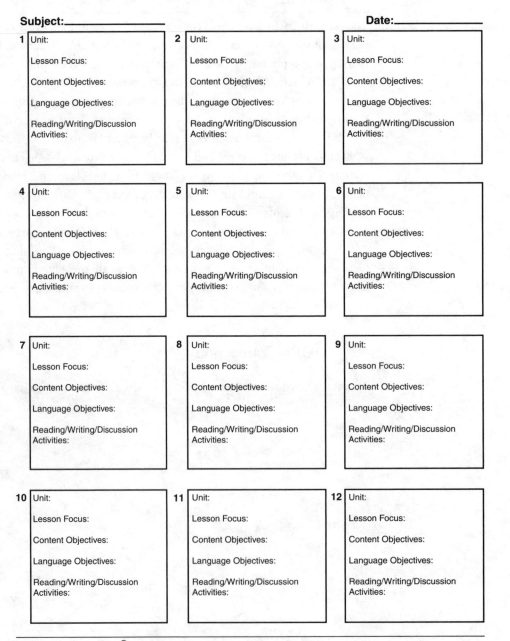

FIGURE 2.2   *SIOP® Planning Flow Chart*

Description:

The purpose of the SIOP® Planning Flow Chart is to create an overview of an entire unit of lessons. It is used to plan a scope and sequence of both language and content objectives, through 12 (or any number) days of instruction. The SIOP® Planning Flow Chart also encourages reading, writing, and discussion (listening and speaking) connections. Teachers who regularly use the SIOP® Planning Flow Chart will begin to see how their language and content objectives can be sequenced to build upon one another throughout a unit.

SIOP® Connection

This particular Preparation activity does not lend itself to specific content or language objectives. For teachers who are very familiar with the SIOP®'s eight components and thirty features, the SIOP® Planning Flow Chart serves as a guide to lesson and unit planning and development.

SIOP® Component: Preparation

Planning SIOP® Lessons

In our work with teachers, we are frequently asked about a usable and effective lesson plan format for the SIOP® Model. Two formats are included in the text, *Making Content Comprehensible for English Learners: The SIOP® Model (2nd ed.)* (Echevarria, Vogt, & Short, 2003). There is a third format in the SIOP® Institute Training Manual, available with participation in a SIOP® Institute (Pearson Achievement Solutions; see www.siopinstitute .net for more information).

We have included another planning format in this book, a lesson plan, created by SIOP® Institute National Faculty, Melissa Castillo and Nicole Teyechea. The one essential difference between Melissa and Nicole's lesson plan from the others we have introduced to you follows: As mentioned previously (see Figure 2.3) the content and language objectives are numbered (e.g., 1, 2, 3, etc.). Now look at the "meaningful activities" and you will see that they correspond to the objectives (1.1, 1.2, 2.1, 2.2, etc.). See also how the assessment recommendations match the numbers for the meaningful activities and the content and language objectives. This is important because teachers need to plan lessons in which the objectives guide the instruction and summative assessment—and the lesson plan format included in this book "force" (gently) them to do this.

Many teachers worry about the time involved in planning SIOP® lessons. Therefore, we encourage all teachers, whether elementary or secondary, to begin slowly—with one subject area (elementary) or academic period (secondary)—when they begin to write SIOP® lesson plans. This is because in the early stages of implementing the SIOP® Model, lesson planning is more involved and time-consuming. With practice, as with all lesson design, SIOP® lessons become easier (and faster) to write. This particular lesson plan format facilitates the process of writing an effective SIOP® content lesson plan without undue stress. Twelve lesson plans have been included in this book. We hope you will find then useful to your work.

FIGURE 2.3 *Lesson Plan*

Key: SW = Students will; TW = Teacher will; SWBAT = Students will be able to..; HOTS = Higher Order Thinking Skills

SIOP® Lesson: *Grade:*

Content Standards:

Key Vocabulary: **Visuals/Resources:**

HOTS:

Connections to Prior Knowledge/Building Background:

Content Objectives:	**Meaningful Activities:**	**Review/Assessment:**
1.	1.1	1.1
	1.2	
2.	2.1	2.1
	2.2	2.2
3.	3.1	3.1
	3.2	3.2
	3.3	
Language Objectives:		
1.	1.1	
	1.2	1.2
2.	2.1	2.2

Wrap-up:

Source: Lesson plan format created by Melissa Castillo and Nicole Teyechea.

SIOP® Component: Preparation

Building Background

Overview of the Building Background Component

Cognitive psychologists have described how learners develop understandings through connections they make among those things they know and have experienced, and those things they are learning. Research supports teachers' explicit activation of students' prior knowledge, and the building of background for those students who may lack prior knowledge of a particular content topic. These linkages of "schemata" help us all learn new information by helping us connect what we know and experience to what we are learning.

All English learners come to school with varied experiences, but not all of their background knowledge matches what they need to know to be successful in U.S. schools. This

mismatch in schemata, in what students have learned and/or experienced, may prevent them from making necessary connections between past and present learning.

It is important therefore, that teachers not only activate students' prior knowledge, but also build background for those who have these gaps in their understandings and background knowledge. This requires teachers to make very explicit connections between what has been taught in the past ("past learning"). Teachers also must include the explicit and purposeful development of vocabulary to foster comprehension.

To enable students to meet grade level content standards, some SIOP® teachers find it beneficial to offer a mini-lesson, or "jump start," to help fill in gaps. It is critical that teachers systematically and purposefully activate students' prior knowledge (determining what they already know and can do related to the topic), and systematically and purposefully develop background information when there is a mismatch or gap.

The Building Background component includes these features:

7. Concepts explicitly linked to students' background experiences.

8. Links explicitly made between past learning and new concepts.

9. Key vocabulary emphasized (e.g., introduced, written, repeated, and highlighted for students to see).

Ideas and Activities for Building Background

Realia, Photos, and Illustrations

COMPONENT: Building Background

Grade Levels: All
Subject Levels: All
Grouping Configurations: Individual, partners, small group, whole class
Materials: A wide variety of realia, photographs, models, and hands-on materials

Description:

The purpose of using realia (real items such as a miner's scale, globe, or apple), photos and/or illustrations, is to enable English learners to develop a clear and precise understanding of an unknown word or unclear concept. Providing hands-on and three-dimensional realia makes key content concepts and key vocabulary come alive.

For example:

1. The teacher introduces key vocabulary words or the class generates a list of words around a particular content topic.

2. The words are introduced and posted on a word wall, chart, or in personal vocabulary dictionaries so that students can refer to them as needed.

3. After introducing the new vocabulary word with realia, illustrations, or photos, students are asked to turn to a partner and use a complete sentence which includes the vocabulary word, referring to the physical object (realia, illustration, or photo) and word wall (or chart or personal dictionary) as needed. Provide beginning English speakers with an illustration or picture (when possible, given the context of the word), and a sentence frame until they are familiar with the procedure and more comfortable speaking with a partner.

An experienced SIOP® teacher suggested that it is helpful to create and maintain a picture file related to the content areas and topics being taught. If you subscribe to magazines or newspapers, watch for photos or illustrations that will enhance your explanation of key concepts and/or vocabulary. Use the Internet to download and print interesting photos and clip art. Store these pictures in a simple file folder with the topic written on the tag. Pull the relevant file(s) when planning SIOP® lessons and you're set; having picture resources quickly available makes planning SIOP® lessons much easier.

SIOP® Connection

Content Objectives:
Students will be able to (SWBAT) . . .

- Use vocabulary related to a content concept (such as transportation).

(continued)

SIOP® Connection (continued)

- Identify realia, photographs, and/or illustrations using the appropriate labels and vocabulary (such as for varied modes of transportation).

Language Objective:

Students will be able to (SWBAT) . . .

- Use the sentence frame:

  "When I go to _____ I travel by _____."

  In the first blank space students will place a vocabulary word related to different places they go (such as to school, the store, or grandmother's). In the second blank students will place vocabulary words that have been introduced for the lesson on transportation (such as car, bike, train, plane, boat, subway, scooter).

KWL Chart

COMPONENT: Building Background

(Ogle, 1986)

> Grade Levels: All
> Subject Levels: All
> Grouping Configurations: Individual, partners, small groups, whole class
> Materials: KWL Chart

Description:

One of the best ways to activate prior knowledge and build background is the familiar KWL (or KWHL) Chart (see Figure 3.1). The purpose of a KWL chart (What We Know/What We Want to Learn (or Wonder About)/What We Have Learned) is to assess students' knowledge about a topic, uncover misconceptions, and most important, allow students input about what they would like to learn about the topic.

Before having students brainstorm each section of the KWL chart, give them some quiet thinking time (approximately 1–2 minutes). Then, for the first box, record all information the students brainstorm, even if it is inaccurate; clarification can take place when the third box is completed, after reading, learning about, and discussing the topic. During the introduction of a lesson or unit, complete the first two sections of the KWL. The third box can be used throughout the unit, adding information each day. Misconceptions can be clarified during discussions and the KWL can be posted so that students can refer back to it as needed.

As an alternative, add a box for "H" for "How We Find Out," before the "What We Have Learned" box. Students use this new box to generate ideas for sources that can be researched to find additional information about the topic.

Unit or Lesson Topic

What We Know	What We Want to Learn	What We Have Learned

FIGURE 3.1 *KWL Chart*

Source: © Ogle, 1986. *The Reading Teacher.*

SIOP® Connection

Content Objectives:

Students will be able to (SWBAT) . . .

- Brainstorm what they already know about (a topic such as animal habitats).
- Identify what they would like to learn about (animals' habitats).
- List what they have learned about (animals' habitats).
- Confirm or disprove information on the chart, while adding newly learned information.

Language Objective:

Students will be able to (SWBAT) . . .

- Use the following sentence frames to state whether information is something they already know, something they want to learn about, or something they learned through the course of instruction.

  "I know that _____."

  "I want to know_____."

  "I learned that _____."

Pretest with a Partner

 **COMPONENT:** Building Background

(Adapted from Angie Medina, Long Beach Unified School District)

Grade Levels: 2–12
Subject Levels: All
Grouping Configuration: Partners
Materials: Copies of pretest and pencils

Description:

Pretest with a Partner allows English learners the opportunity to preview at the beginning of the lesson or unit the material that will be assessed at its conclusion. The teacher distributes one pretest and one pencil to each set of partners. The pretest should be similar or identical to the posttest that will be administered at the end of the lesson or unit. The students pass the pretest and the pencil back and forth between one another, first reading the question aloud, then discussing the possible answer, and once they come to a consensus, writing the answer on the pretest. They continue in this manner until all questions are answered. This activity provides an opportunity for the students to share any background knowledge they have with a partner, while the teacher is able to circulate around the room to assess the background knowledge that is already in place, and become aware of any areas where knowledge is lacking.

SIOP® Connection

Content Objectives:

Students will be able to (SWBAT) . . .

- Preview the content of (topic) by taking a pretest with a partner.
- Share knowledge while making predictions and asking questions about pretest items of which they are unsure.

Language Objective:

Students will be able to (SWBAT) . . .

- Use questioning and clarifying terms to initiate discussion with a partner:

    "Do you know anything about that?"

    "I'm not sure about the answer, but I do know _____."

    "I think the answer might be _____, because I learned _____."

Backwards Book Walk

SIOP® COMPONENT: Building Background

(Adapted from Bonnie Bishop, Long Beach Unified School District)

Grade Levels: 2–12
Subject Levels: Science, Social Studies, English Language Development (ELD)
Grouping Configurations: Individual, partners, small groups, whole class
Materials: Nonfiction text

Description:

The purpose of a Backwards Book Walk is to familiarize students with a nonfiction text before they begin to read it independently. It begins with the conclusion, so students understand the overall meaning of the text (book or chapter) before looking at the bits and pieces. After reading the conclusion, the students continue in a backwards manner, reading headings, captions, and keywords. This provides students with an introduction to important vocabulary so they will better comprehend the text information. After the entire chapter has been reviewed, students are asked to guess the title of the text. Allow quiet thinking time and then have students share thoughts with their partners, before the partners share with the class. This activity reverses the process of the typical picture or text walk, motivating students through the novelty of something new while demonstrating a technique for pre-reading a nonfiction text.

SIOP® Connection

Content Objectives:

Students will be able to (SWBAT) . . .

- Read the conclusion of a text and use textual features to make predictions about what they will learn while reading the text.
- Add to or change their predictions while reading the text.

Language Objective:

Students will be able to (SWBAT) . . .

- Use the following sentence frames after doing a backwards walk through a book or chapter:

    "The conclusion and other text features makes me think that we are going to learn _____."

    "We might learn about _____."

    "I don't think this chapter will be about _____."

Go to Your Corner

SIOP® SHELTERED INSTRUCTION OBSERVATION PROTOCOL

COMPONENT: Building Background

(RWCT Project of the International Reading Association)

Grade Levels: All

Subject Levels: All

Grouping Configurations: Partners, small groups, whole class

Materials: Labels for corners' topics and illustrations for each, if possible

Description:

The purpose of Go to Your Corner is to give students an opportunity to share their knowledge about a topic. It also lets students practice their paraphrasing skills. Choose a topic that has at least four possible dimensions and assign each dimension to a specific corner of the room. This works best if the corners are labeled and a picture of the topic included. Students move to a particular corner based on interest or by assigning each student a word or picture related to one of the corners. Once in their corners, students pair with a partner and explain why they chose that corner. After ample time to talk, students from each corner share their reasons with the entire class. This can be charted if desired.

For example, supply each student with an index card with a picture and/or word that describes one of four Native American tribes. The students mix around the room sharing and trading their index cards with each other. When the teacher calls "Freeze," the students move to the corner where the tribe on their card is represented. Once students are assembled in one of the four corners, they share their picture/word cards with each other, and the group comes to consensus about whether the picture/word is related to their particular tribe. If a student is not in the correct corner, the other students help direct him or her to the appropriate tribe. This activity has many possibilities and can be carried into a discussion, writing assignment, or graphic organizer that classifies information about each dimension of the topic.

SIOP® Connection

Content Objective:

Students will be able to (SWBAT) . . .

- Classify information about four different Native American tribes.

Language Objective:

Students will be able to (SWBAT) . . .

- Explain the connection between a picture/word on an index card and the particular Native American tribe that it describes, using the following prompts:

    "This is a word related to the _____ tribe because they _____."

    "This is a picture related to the _____ tribe because they _____."

The Insert Method

SIOP® COMPONENT: Building Background

(RWCT Project of the International Reading Association)

Grade Levels: 3–12
Subject Levels: All
Grouping Configuration: Partners, Small Groups, Whole Class, Individual
Materials: Informational or expository text duplicated on paper students can write on

Description:

In partners, students read a nonfiction article using the following coding system, inserting the codes directly into the text they are reading:

- A check (√) mark indicates a concept or fact that is already known by the students.
- A question (?) mark indicates a concept or fact that is confusing or not understood.
- An exclamation mark (!) indicates something that is new, unusual or surprising.
- A (+) indicates an idea or concept that is new to the reader.

When the partners have concluded reading and marking the text, they share their markings with another set of partners. As misconceptions or misunderstandings are cleared up, the question mark is replaced with an asterisk (*). Following this small group work, the text is discussed with the teacher and the whole class.

SIOP® Connection

Content Objectives:

Students will be able to (SWBAT) . . .

- Use a coding system while reading a nonfiction text to identify concepts or facts that are familiar, those that are confusing, and those that are new, unusual, or surprising.
- Clarify misconceptions and misunderstandings about a text while working with group members.

Language Objectives:

Students will be able to (SWBAT) . . .

- Ask questions about concepts and facts that are confusing.
- Read and discuss with group members a piece of nonfiction text.

Student Journals

SIOP® COMPONENT: **Building Background**

Grade Levels: 1–12
Subject Levels: All
Grouping Configurations: Individual, partners, small groups, whole class
Materials: Individual composition books or stapled journals (binder paper stapled with construction paper cover)

Description:

Student Journals allow students to reflect back on previous learning and build on that knowledge while reading and writing about a topic. Journals also help the teacher better understand what the students are learning (or remembering) from a lesson or unit. Student journal writing (or drawing for very young children and beginning English speakers) can be completed before, during, and/or after a lesson or unit. The key to this activity is encouraging students to return to previous entries to remember and build on information. Student Journals have more impact if the teacher writes occasional reactions to student entries.

   As an example, students can review earlier journal entries to access their background knowledge about the life cycle of a butterfly. After reading through what they learned previously, the students share with a partner and then bring the information into a whole class discussion. This previous learning becomes the foundation for a new lesson on the life cycle of a frog. Student comprehension of life cycles is enhanced by the connections they make between the two topics.

SIOP® Connection

Content Objective:

Students will be able to (SWBAT) . . .

  • Connect their knowledge of the life cycle of a butterfly to the life cycle of a frog.

Language Objective:

Students will be able to (SWBAT) . . .

  • Make predictions and explain the connection between their previous learning and the new content to be learned by using the word "because:"

     "I think that the frog's life cycle will _____ because the butterfly's life cycle _____ ."

     "I think that the frog _____ because the butterfly _____ ."

Personal Dictionaries

SIOP®
SHELTERED INSTRUCTION
OBSERVATION PROTOCOL

COMPONENT: Building Background

Grade Levels: All
Subject Levels: All
Grouping Configurations: Individual, partners, small groups, whole class
Materials: Individual composition books or stapled journals (binder paper stapled with construction paper cover)

Description:

The purpose of Personal Dictionaries is to support students' learning of key vocabulary. Students create the dictionaries as individual vocabulary and spelling resources, adding unknown words they come across while reading. The teacher works with students to clarify the meanings of the new words.

The words in the dictionaries can be categorized in alphabetical order, by subject, sound, morphological structure (such as past tense words), or by content and topic. Secondary teachers can have students create personal word dictionaries that include content specific vocabulary. Very young children and beginning English speakers are encouraged to use simple illustrations to represent words they are learning. In K-1, words can come from big books through a shared reading experience.

SIOP® Connection

Content Objectives:

Students will be able to (SWBAT) . . .

- Select and define words for ongoing vocabulary learning.
- Make connections between previously learned vocabulary and vocabulary found in a new lesson/text.

Language Objectives:

Students will be able to (SWBAT) . . .

- Write (or draw) a definition (or related meaning) for each new vocabulary word selected from text.
- Describe vocabulary connections using the following prompts:

    "I remember this word from when we read about _____."

    "I remember what this word means from when we read about _____."

    "I remember putting this word in my dictionary when we read about _____."

Signal Words

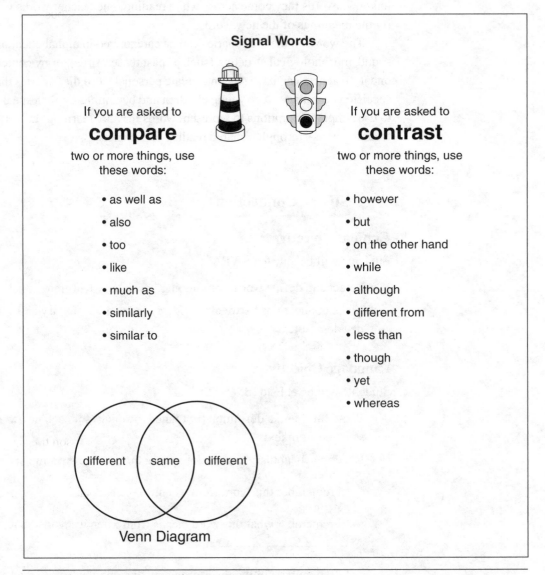

COMPONENT: Building Background

(Sarah Russell, ESL teacher, Hug High School, Washoe County School District)

Grade Levels: 3–12

Subject Levels: All

Grouping Configurations: Independent writing and reading

Materials: Signal Word Posters (see Figure 3.2–3.5)

Description:

Sarah Russell, a high school ESL teacher in Reno, NV created the posters that you see in Figures 3.2–3.5. She discovered her English learners were having difficulty reading and

Signal Words

If you are asked to

compare

two or more things, use these words:

- as well as
- also
- too
- like
- much as
- similarly
- similar to

If you are asked to

contrast

two or more things, use these words:

- however
- but
- on the other hand
- while
- although
- different from
- less than
- though
- yet
- whereas

different   same   different

Venn Diagram

FIGURE 3.2 *Signal Words: Compare/Contrast*

Sarah Russell, Hug High School, Washoe County School District

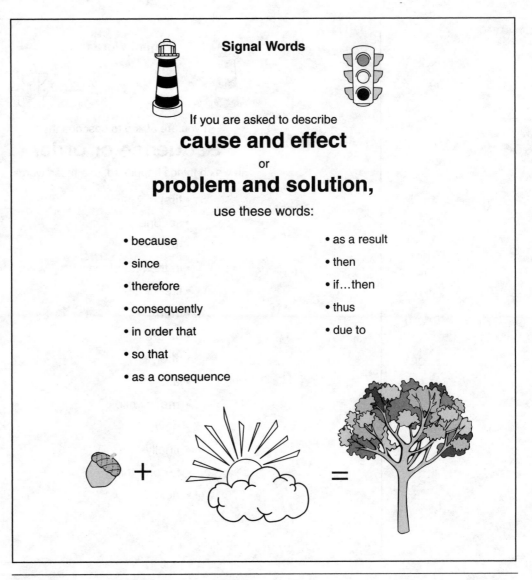

FIGURE 3.3 *Signal Words: Cause and Effect*

Sarah Russell, Hug High School, Washoe County School District

writing because of the varied types of text structure found in textbooks (e.g., compare/contrast, sequence, description, cause/effect). Sarah created a list of words and phrases that "signal" the four types of text structure and made them into posters which she hangs in her classroom. Her English learners routinely refer to the posters while reading and writing. The content and language objectives below are from a lesson that Sarah teaches. Note that younger English learners will also benefit from instruction in and exposure to these signal words.

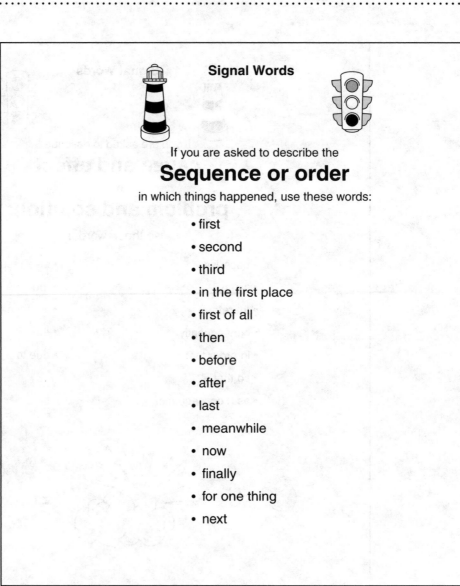

Signal Words

If you are asked to describe the

Sequence or order

in which things happened, use these words:

- first
- second
- third
- in the first place
- first of all
- then
- before
- after
- last
- meanwhile
- now
- finally
- for one thing
- next

FIGURE 3.4 *Signal Words: Sequence or Order*

Sarah Russell, Hug High School, Washoe County School District

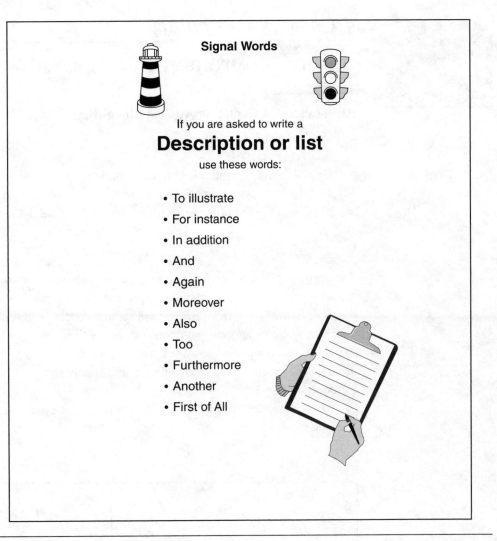

FIGURE 3.5 *Signal Words: Description or List*

Sarah Russell, Hug High School, Washoe County School District

SIOP® Connection

Content Objective:

(For a lesson on events leading up to the Civil War) Students will be able to (SWBAT) . . .

- Compare and contrast the North and South's positions in the weeks preceding the first battle of the Civil War.

Language Objective:

Students will be able to (SWBAT) . . .

- Select the appropriate signal words for comparing and contrasting the North and South's positions.

- Write five sentences about the North and South's positions in the weeks preceding the first battle of the Civil War.

4-Corners Vocabulary

SHELTERED INSTRUCTION
SIOP®
OBSERVATION PROTOCOL

COMPONENT: Building Background

(Deborah Short, Center for Applied Linguistics)

Grade Levels: All

Subject Levels: All

Grouping Configurations: Partners, small groups, whole class

Materials: Large piece of chart paper folded in fourths; students may also fold an 8-1/2 × 11 sheet of paper in fourths for a personal 4-Corners Vocabulary activity.

Description:

The purpose of 4-Corners Vocabulary is to enable students to contextualize words by creating a chart with an illustration (representing the word), a sentence (that includes the word), a definition (of the word), and the actual vocabulary word. The teacher may create the chart, while upper grade students may create their own. Fold the chart paper in fourths so that students can only view one corner at a time. Start with the illustration, then the definition, then the contextualized sentence, and finally show the class the actual vocabulary word (see Figure 3.6).

Once completed, the 4-Corners Vocabulary chart can be posted on the wall for further reference.

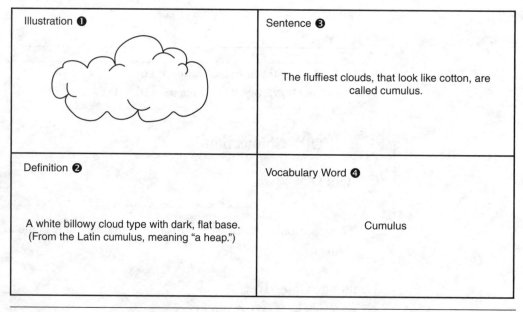

FIGURE 3.6 *4-Corners Vocabulary*

SIOP® Connection

Content Objective:

Students will be able to (SWBAT) . . .

- Use an illustration, a definition, and a contextualized sentence to determine (a matching vocabulary word).

Language Objectives:

Students will be able to (SWBAT) . . .

- Read a contextualized sentence that includes (a vocabulary word).
- Read the definition for (a vocabulary word).

Identifying and Using Cognates to Teach English Vocabulary

SIOP® SHELTERED INSTRUCTION OBSERVATION PROTOCOL

COMPONENT: Building Background

Grade Levels: All
Subject Levels: All
Grouping Configurations: Individual, partners, small groups, whole class
Materials: A list of Spanish cognates; a list of Latin and Greek roots will also be helpful

Description:

A cognate is a word related in meaning and form to a word in another language because the words have the same historical source. For example, the Romance languages, including French, Spanish, Italian, Portuguese, and Romanian, are each derived from Latin. Cognates are generally easy to recognize because they are spelled similarly. English and Spanish have many cognates, and for Spanish-speaking students learning new content, understanding cognates helps them make connections to what they already know. Figure 3.7 contains examples of the many cognates found in English and Spanish.

FIGURE 3.7 *Examples of Cognates*

English	Spanish	Meaning
capital	capital	A city or town in which government leaders and others meet and work on behalf of a state, province, or country.
cause	causa	A person or thing that makes something happen.
artifact	artefacto	An object that is made and used by a particular group of people.
colony	colonia	A place that is ruled by another country.
communication	comunicacion	Sharing ideas with others orally or in writing.
community	comunidad	A place where people live and work together.
congress	congreso	A country's lawmakers.
conservation	conservacion	Working to save natural resources to make them last longer.
consumer	consumidor	A person who buys and uses goods and services.
continent	continente	One of the largest bodies of land on the Earth.
desert	desierto	A dry place; very little rain falls in a desert.
diagram	diagrama	An illustration or flow chart that provides information about how something works.
geography	geografia	The study of the Earth and its people.
globe	globo	A model of the Earth.
group	grupo	A number of people doing an activity together.
history	historia	Events that have occurred in the past.
independence	independencia	The freedom of people to choose their own government.
invention	invencion	Something that has been created for the first time.
island	isla	Land that has water all around it.
leader	lider	A person who helps a group plan what to do.

We must be careful of false cognates (i.e. Spanish and English words that look very similar but do not mean the same thing) (see Figure 3.8).

FIGURE 3.8 *Examples of False Cognates*

English	Spanish
agenda	orden del dia
appointment book	agenda
disturb	molestar
molest	accion indebido (sexual connotations)
embarrassed	avergonzado/a
pregnant	embarazada
excited	ansioso, nervioso, contento
	excitado/s (sexual connotations)
library	biblioteca
book store	libreria
minutes (from meeting)	acta (de una reunion)
portable	poratil
sympathy	pesame, condolencia
friendliness, congeniality	simpatia

Source: © 2006 Pearson Achievement Solutions, a division of Pearson Education. All rights reserved.

SIOP® Connection

Content Objectives:

Students will be able to (SWBAT) . . .

- Recognize cognates in English that share the same roots as in their native language (if appropriate).
- Determine the difference between cognates and false cognates in Spanish and English. (This objective applies to students whose L1 is Spanish).

Language Objective:

Students will be able to (SWBAT) . . .

- Use their knowledge of cognates to read and then define words in English.

Surprise Book

SHELTERED INSTRUCTION
SIOP®
OBSERVATION · PROTOCOL

COMPONENT: Building Background

(Adapted from Bonnie Bishop, Long Beach Unified School District)

Grade Levels: K–5
Subject Levels: All
Grouping Configurations: Whole class
Approximate Time: Can vary from 5–10 minutes (depending on age and English proficiency of students)
Materials: Interesting children's book; wrapping paper

Description:

Using the Surprise Book activity at the beginning of a unit activates students' background knowledge, while sparking their interest through the element of surprise. Choose a book that represents the unit theme and has good visuals on the cover, and wrap the book in plain butcher or chart paper so that no part of the book is visible. At the beginning of the unit present the wrapped book to the class. Tell the students they will slowly unwrap the book, taking small pieces of paper off one at a time. Model the tearing away of the pieces and ask students to take turns removing bits of the paper. As the paper is slowly torn away revealing the pictures on the cover, encourage students to make predictions about the book's topic or theme. Their ideas will come together piece by piece and at the end of the process they will know the theme of their next lesson or unit of study.

SIOP® Connection

Content Objective:

Students will be able to (SWBAT) . . .

- Make connections between their background knowledge and (the topic) of the Surprise Book.

Language Objective:

Students will be able to (SWBAT) . . .

- Speak in the future tense to predict what their next lesson or unit of study will be using the following sentence frames:

  "I think we *will* learn about _____."

  "I think we *are going* to study _____."

  "I think this book *will be* about _____."

The SIOP® Model: Building Background

Lesson Plans

The following lesson plans (see Figure 3.9–3.10) include the Student Journal activity (p. 34). While these lessons incorporate all eight SIOP® Components, the emphasis is on Building Background. The teacher will explicitly provide students with background experiences using literature books and video clips. Connections between past learning and new concepts are made through questioning and quick-write techniques. Key vocabulary is emphasized in context as the teacher introduces the content concept (frogs) that is the focus of the lesson. Students are expected to apply vocabulary as they practice, demonstrating their understanding of the content concepts.

Keep in mind that these lesson plans serve as examples. Depending on the grade level you teach and state standards, substitute the appropriate literature selections, videos, resources, and objectives. These examples are intended to demonstrate how to incorporate the Building Background component of the SIOP® Model into a lesson plan.

FIGURE 3.9 *Elementary Lesson Plan for Building Background*

Key: SW = Students will; TW = Teacher will; SWBAT = Students will be able to . . . ; HOTS = Higher Order Thinking Skills

SIOP® Lesson: Life Cycles	Grade: 2

Content Standard: Strand 3 Life Cycles
Concept 2: Understand the life cycles of plants and animals
PO1. Describe the life cycle of various amphibians
Grade 2

Key Vocabulary: Similar, different, metamorphasis, embryo, tadpole, & cells **HOTS:** Why is it important to know about plant and animal life cycles?	**Visuals/Resources/Supplementary Materials:** Overhead of Butterfly Cycle, Overhead of Frog Life Cycle Student Journals, Text: "The Metamorphosis: From Tadpole to Frog"

Connections to Prior Knowledge/Building Background (20 min.):
SW review in their science journals previous notes and quick-writes on the butterfly cycle.
SW do a quick-write answering the following questions in their journals:

1. What does the term metamorphosis mean? (link to past learning)
2. Where have you seen butterflies outside of school?
3. What are the stages of the life cycle of a butterfly? Draw and label each.

SW turn to a partner and share their quick-writes and illustrations.

Content Objective:	**Meaningful Activities:**	**Review/Assessment:**
1. SWBAT demonstrate knowledge of the life cycle of an amphibian (frog) by illustrating and labeling the stages.	**1.1** TW review on the overhead the stages of the life cycle of the butterfly emphasizing the term *Metamorphosis*.	
	1.2 TW read "The Metamorphosis: From Tadpole to Frog".	
	1.3 SW, in a group, illustrate and label each stage of the life cycle of a frog using a piece of chart paper including key vocabulary.	**1.3** Students' posters including the word *metamorphasis, embryo, tad*pole and *cells*.

(continued)

FIGURE 3.9 *Elementary Lesson Plan for Building Background* *(continued)*

Language Objective:		
2. SWBAT demonstrate analysis of the life cycle of an amphibian (frog) by writing a summary explaining the cycle using cloze sentences.	**2.1** SW complete the following sentence starters (in their journals): The Life cycle begins with an egg which forms into an _____. After 21 days the _____ then becomes a _____ which has a long tail and lives in the water. Finally, as the tail becomes smaller and the legs get longer you have _____.	**2.1** SW share their writing with a partner and with the teacher.

Wrap-up: Stand up/sit down for True/False

TW make a statement; if true students stand; if false they stay seated.

SW then justify their responses by completing the following sentences: "The statement is true because . . ." "The statement is false because . . ."

Examples of True/False statements:

The life cycle of a frog and the life cycle of the butterfly both have four stages.

Both frogs and butterflies go through metamorphosis.

Both frogs and butterflies begin as a single egg.

Source: Lesson plan created by Melissa Castillo and Nicole Teyechea. Lesson content by Melissa Castillo and Kendra Moreno.

FIGURE 3.10 *Secondary Lesson Plan for Building Background*

Key: SW = Students will; TW = Teacher will; SWBAT = Students will be able to . . .; HOTS = Higher Order Thinking Skills

SIOP® Lesson: Life Cycles   *Grade: 8*

Content Standard: Concept 4: Life Science
PO 1: Understands how species depend on one another and the environment for survival.

Key Vocabulary: amphibian, displace, ecology, food web, habitat, species	**Visuals/Resources:** poster paint, markers, poster board, books and magazines on frogs and toads and encyclopedias;
HOTS: Does your frog play a role in the food chain? How? How would the decline of your frog affect the food chain?	Video: Frogs: Facts and Folklore; Student journals

Connections to Prior Knowledge/Building Background (20 min.):

SW view a short video clip on frogs (Facts and Folklore)

SW answer the following questions in their journals:

1. What's the difference between frogs and toads?

2. How might frogs be helpful in medical studies?

3. Where did we get the expression "to have a frog in your throat?"

4. What are the implications of the frog population crash?

SW will share one response with a partner.

Content Objectives:	**Meaningful Activities:**	**Review/Assessment:**
1. SWBAT demonstrate knowledge of how species (frogs) depend on one another and their environment by choosing one species from their environment, and identifying where, why and how they depend on their environment.	**1.1** TW will introduce on the overhead an "American Frog" picture (or any example teacher chooses), and share with students using key vocabulary its characteristics and the environment the species lives in.	

(continued)

FIGURE 3.10 *Secondary Lesson Plan for Building Background* *(continued)*

	1.2 SW then choose one species from a list of frogs in their state to research on the Internet and available encyclopedias. SW will complete fact sheet including *what, where, why* and *how.*	**1.2** SW will use the appropriate key vocabulary to define their chosen frog. For example: Where the frogs *habitat* can be found What part they play in the food *web*
2. SWBAT demonstrate comprehension of how species (frogs) depend on one another and their environment by labeling and illustrating one species and its surrounding habitat in small groups.	**2.1** SW in their small groups using poster board identify their species and list its characteristics and habitat.	**2.1** Student poster will include frog facts: size, color, habitat and diet—what a frog eats and what eats the frog.
Language Objective: **1.** SWBAT demonstrate evaluation of how species (frogs) depend on one another and their environment by writing a summary explaining their species and how it is suited to its habitat.	**1.1** SW in their journals use their frog facts to write a one paragraph summary completing the following sentence starters (examples): The _____ frog is found in _____. It measures _____ and its color is _____. The _____ eats _____. It is food for _____ and can be _____.	**1.1** Student journals

Wrap-up:
SW, in their groups, present their posters in a jigsaw activity.

Source: Lesson plan created by Melissa Castillo and Nicole Teyechea. Lesson content by Melissa Castillo and Kendra Moreno.

chapter 4

Comprehensible Input

Overview of Comprehensible Input Component

Think back to when you were in a high school physics, chemistry, French or any other challenging class you took. Remember how you felt when you "got it?" Now reflect on those times when, despite teacher explanations, you just didn't "get" what you were supposed to be learning. How did you feel? Did your teacher do something that further muddled your already cloudy understanding? What could the teacher have done to make the content concepts more clear?

For English learners to understand your instruction, it is imperative that you implement techniques to improve comprehensibility. It is not enough to speak loudly—your students will hear you very well, but still may not understand what you're saying. You need to speak at an appropriate pace (not too fast or too slow, which results in unnatural speech), enunciate clearly, and use gestures and body language, when appropriate, to reinforce your points.

It is also important that you make your explanations very clear regarding what students are to do and how they are to do it. When steps to processes and procedures are written, orally presented, and modeled, English learners (and other students) will be likely to meet their content and language objectives. We cannot expect ELs to master new content learning by just listening; They need demonstrations, photos, illustrations, and models to make sense of the words you are speaking. And this is what it means to provide input that is comprehensible.

The Comprehensible Input component includes these features:

10. Speech appropriate for student proficiency levels (e.g., slower rate, enunciation, and simple sentence for beginners).

11. Clear explanation of academic tasks.

12. A variety of techniques to make content concepts clear (e.g., modeling, visuals, hands-on activities, demonstrations, gestures, body language).

Ideas and Activities for Providing Comprehensible Input

Identifying Levels of Second Language Acquisition

SIOP® SHELTERED INSTRUCTION OBSERVATION PROTOCOL **COMPONENT:** Comprehensible Input

Grade Levels: All
Subject Areas: All
Grouping Configuration: None (Teacher assessment)
Approximate Time Involved: On-going process for every lesson
Materials: None

Description:

It is very important that teachers determine the English language acquisition levels of their students. Once ascertained, teachers can make content comprehensible based on each student's language needs. Teachers can also encourage students to increase their English proficiency by providing activities and opportunities that promote the frequent use of English.

The following stages of language acquisition are fluid; English learners (ELs) don't move in concrete steps from one stage to the other. It is helpful for teachers to understand how their students are progressing in acquiring English, and how they might respond to varying classroom instruction. Note that the number of stages and the labels for the stages may vary regionally. What is important to remember is that learning a language is a process and that the more ELs use English (which includes listening to conventional English usage), the more proficient they will become.

Beginning (Pre-Production)

English learners in this stage have little comprehension of oral and written English, and are unable to produce much, if any, English. Teachers should provide abundant listening opportunities, use physical gestures and movements to convey meaning, and include a great deal of context for shared reading and writing. If possible, partner beginning English speakers with others who speak the same primary language, keeping in mind that students may understand more than they can orally communicate.

Beginning (Early Production)

In this stage ELs have limited English comprehension but can now give one or two word oral responses. For students learning to read in English, teachers can use predictable and patterned books, encouraging them to label and manipulate pictures, and fill in cloze sentences that are highly contextualized.

Beginning (Early Speech Emergence)

English learners can speak in simple sentences and comprehend highly contextualized oral and written information. Teachers can expect these students to respond to simple open-ended questions, and should continue to provide sufficient language development opportunities, including many activities that require students to read, write, listen, and speak. Students should be encouraged to talk and write about personal experiences.

Intermediate (Early)

Students at this stage have some proficiency in communicating simple ideas and comprehend contextualized information. Teachers should continue to develop and extend sight word vocabulary, encouraging English learners to expand on simple responses while developing critical thinking skills. These students should practice important grammatical structures to further their ability to generate and communicate ideas.

Intermediate

At this stage ELs have proficiency in communicating ideas and comprehending contextualized information in English. Teachers should provide explicit instruction in figurative language, making predictions, using text features to read a book, and in English grammar. These students can participate in generative activities that promote higher levels of thinking.

Early Advanced

These English learners can communicate well, have good comprehension of information, and have adequate vocabulary to achieve academically. Teachers should provide for a variety of realistic writing and speaking opportunities, exposing these students to many different genres, more advanced grammatical structures, and activities to practice further critical thinking skills.

Advanced

Students at this stage have near native speech fluency, very good comprehension of information in English, and expanded vocabulary to achieve academically. These students can lead group discussions, and should be given opportunities to do presentations and produce oral and written forms of communication. Teachers should continue to provide explicit grammar instruction.

Examples of divergent responses from students at varied levels of English proficiency include:

- *Beginning:* "Brown bear."
- *Early Intermediate:* "The bear is brown. It has claws."
- *Intermediate:* "The bear has thick fur and sharp claws."
- *Early Advanced:* "The bear isn't a predator even though it has sharp claws and teeth."
- *Advanced:* "Before they hibernate for the winter, brown bears give birth to cubs."
  (California Reading and Literature Project)

Please remember that students at lower levels of English proficiency are not necessarily functioning at lower levels of cognitive ability. Frequently these students are able to use higher level thinking skills in their primary language but have a more difficult time understanding academic content and expressing their knowledge in English.

SIOP® Connection

Information about students' levels of English proficiency does not lend itself to specific content and language objectives. It is information for teachers to use when planning instruction that provides appropriate comprehensible input for English learners with varying levels of English proficiency

Move It!

SIOP® SHELTERED INSTRUCTION OBSERVATION PROTOCOL

COMPONENT: Comprehensible Input

(Adapted from Asher, 1982)

Grade Levels: All (movements may be adjusted to age, developmental, and language proficiency levels of students)
Subject Areas: All
Grouping Configurations: Individual, partners, small group, whole class
Approximate Time Involved: Used at beginning of lesson to build background knowledge, clarify meaning during lesson input, and/or to review concepts
Materials: None

Description:

Move It! enables the teacher and students to respond with physicality, by moving their bodies, to a lesson. Movement appeals to all, but especially to kinesthetic learners . . . and those who don't yet have the English proficiency to express themselves clearly. The teacher can use hands, facial expressions, or whole body movement to illustrate key points in the lesson. The children then repeat the actions to make meaning of new words or concepts.

For example, when teaching about orbit, rotation, and revolution of the planets, the teacher rotates and revolves her body around a light bulb which represents the sun. The students will then get a chance to rotate, revolve, and orbit around the "sun." Or students can move their hands like an "alligator," chomping on the biggest piece when a teacher is teaching concepts of greater than and less than in a math lesson. Move It! is fun and useful for all students; however it is vital for newcomer students with beginning English language proficiency.

Signals are also great for student interaction within a lesson. Using hand signals for yes/no, true/false, I understand/I sort of understand/I don't understand responses, will help teachers monitor the progress of ELs in order to make important decisions about how to proceed with lesson delivery.

SIOP® Connection

Content Objective:

Students will be able to (SWBAT) . . .

- Demonstrate understanding of (a concept, such as if a number is greater than or less than another number) by using an appropriate hand signal.

(continued)

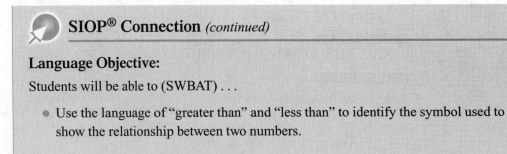

SIOP® Connection *(continued)*

Language Objective:

Students will be able to (SWBAT) . . .

- Use the language of "greater than" and "less than" to identify the symbol used to show the relationship between two numbers.

  "_____ is greater than _____."

  "_____ is less than _____."

Vocabulary Cards and Flip Books

 COMPONENT: Comprehensible Input

Grade Levels: All
Subject Areas: All
Grouping Configuration: Small group or whole class
Approximate Time Involved: 30 minutes
Materials: 8.5 × 11″ sheets of paper; index cards of any size

Description:

Teachers often use vocabulary cards for review. The cards can however, also be used to introduce or frontload vocabulary at the beginning of a lesson. This process helps students build on background knowledge and increase comprehension of the lesson or unit being studied.

There are many ways to make vocabulary cards, and they can include sections for the word, picture, and/or definition. Cards can also provide a place to use the word in a sentence. As a class spends time negotiating the meanings of key words before a lesson, they become familiar with the concepts that will be discussed throughout the unit.

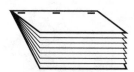

FIGURE 4.1
Vocabulary Flip Book
Source: © 2006 Pearson Achievement Solutions, a division of Pearson Education. All right reserved.

Students can also make flip books with 8.5″ × 11″ pieces of paper displaying the vocabulary information. To make flip books, line up and arrange the paper so that about an inch of each piece can be seen. Fold all the papers in half and put a paper clip on each folded half. Cut along the fold and staple each section along the top (see Figure 4.1). You will now have two flipbooks.

As an example, students could create an eight-layer flip book; the first layer represents the title Taxonomy, and the subsequent seven layers represent the order of classification from smallest to largest: species, genus, family, order, class, phylum, kingdom. The flip book pages increase in size, just as the areas of classification do: For the taxonomy example, *kingdom* is written on the largest page of the flip book.

> ### 🧭 SIOP® Connection
>
> **Content Objective:**
>
> Students will be able to (SWBAT) . . .
>
> - Identify and describe (insert appropriate number) areas of classification within a taxonomy.
>
> **Language Objectives:**
>
> Students will be able to (SWBAT) . . .
>
> - Use comparative and superlative words to describe the order and size in a taxonomy: largest, larger, large, small, smaller, and smallest.
> - Use ordinal numbers (first through eighth) to decide on which page of the flip book each classification should be placed.

Homographs, Homophones, and Synonyms

SIOP® COMPONENT: Comprehensible Input

Grade Levels: 2–12
Subject Areas: Language Arts
Grouping Configuration: Individual, small group, whole class
Approximate Time Involved: On-going
Materials: Word lists of homophones, homographs, and synonyms

Description:

English learners benefit from explicit instruction of homographs, homophones, and synonyms. Maintain a list of homographs (phrases which include words that are spelled the same but have different meanings, like *duck under a gate,* a *duck in the pond*), homophones (words that sound the same but have different meanings and spellings, such as *sale and sail*), and synonyms (different words that share the same meaning such as *talk/speak* and *sadness/sorrow*). Posting these words gives students access to "tricky" words that can be difficult for students learning English, and simple illustrations can serve as helpful mnemonics. Students can also organize these words in personal dictionaries or vocabulary notebooks.

✎ SIOP® Connection

Content Objective:

Students will be able to (SWBAT) . . .

- Classify words as homographs, homophones, or synonyms.

Language Objectives:

Students will be able to (SWBAT) . . .

- Demonstrate understanding that even though words may sound the same or share the same spelling, they may have different meanings.
- Use sentence structures that compare and contrast word pairs to determine if the words are synonyms, homographs, or homophones.

  "_____ and _____ have the same meaning. They are synonyms."

  "_____ and _____ are spelled the same but they have different meanings. They are homographs."

  "_____ and _____ sound the same but have different meanings and spellings. They are homophones."

Idiom Match-Up

SIOP® SHELTERED INSTRUCTION OBSERVATION PROTOCOL | **COMPONENT:** Comprehensible Input

Grade Levels: 3–8
Subject Areas: Language Arts
Grouping Configuration: Partners
Approximate Time Involved: 1.5 hours to create game; students can complete the game in 10–15 minutes
Materials: List of English idioms; cardboard, marking pens

Description:

Idioms and idiomatic expressions can cause difficulty for English learners. Have students record idioms in a separate section of their personal dictionary or vocabulary notebook, and use simple illustrations to remember the words. A fun way for ELs to practice their understanding of idioms is to play an idiom match-up game. Create a game board (colored poster board or colored file folder) and game cards (tag board cut into 2″ × 2″ squares). Divide the poster board into 2″ × 2″ squares with a marking pen, leaving space at the top for the game's name and playing directions. In each square, write an idiom or idiomatic expression. On each 2″ × 2″ card, write the meaning of the idiom. Ask student pairs to match the meaning to the idiom. Illustrating the literal meanings of the idioms (e.g., a person who is frozen in an ice cube for the expression "Freeze!"), and matching these to the idiomatic meanings helps students remember their meanings. Students might also enjoy sharing some idioms from their native languages.

Following are some common English idioms and their meanings:

Idiom	Meaning
Shake a leg!	Hurry!
You'll catch more flies with sugar than vinegar.	Act nicely; don't be mean.
Hop to it!	Get started on what you need to do.
Freeze!	Do not move.
He's off the wall.	He behaves strangely.
She's over the top.	Her actions go beyond what people expect.
If you can't stand the heat, get out of the kitchen!	Leave if you are uncomfortable with what people are saying or doing.
He has an eye for the girls.	He likes to flirt with pretty girls.
She has an eye for fashion.	She dresses very well.

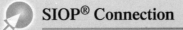

SIOP® Connection

Content Objective:

Students will be able to (SWBAT) . . .

- Match English idiomatic expressions with their meanings.

Language Objective:

Students will be able to (SWBAT) . . .

- Read and explain orally to a partner the meaning of English idiomatic expressions.

Taped Texts for Scaffolding

COMPONENT: Comprehensible Input

Grade Levels: All
Subject Areas: All
Grouping Configuration: Individual, partner, small group, whole class
Approximate Time Involved: Depends on text; recording can be time-consuming, but the tape can be used repeatedly once completed.
Materials: Tape recorder or other recording device; expository or narrative texts

Description:

Taping text is an effective way to make content comprehensible. The reader (teacher, student, or other individual) should take special care to use speech appropriate for student proficiency levels, use a slower reading rate, and clearly enunciate words. The reader adapts the text by finding synonyms for difficult words and deleting superfluous language, idioms, and figurative expressions that may confuse English language learners. Careful intonation and use of inflection for dialogue makes these parts of the text more understandable. Using students or other people for readers provides varied inflections and intonations, expanding the voices heard speaking English in the classroom. Most important, ELs can listen to the text repeatedly to improve comprehension and increase their English proficiency.

SIOP® Connection

Content Objective:

Students will be able to (SWBAT) . . .

- Identify three key concepts related to _____ (topic) after listening to _____ (story, article, or chapter).

Language Objective:

Students will be able to (SWBAT) . . .

- Orally explain to a partner why he or she thinks the identified three concepts are the most important in the (story, article, or chapter).

Every Student Gets a Chance

COMPONENT: Comprehensible Input

Grade Levels: 2–12

Subject Areas: All

Grouping Configuration: Small group, whole class

Approximate Time Involved: 5 minutes

Materials: Chalk, white board, or chart paper

Description:

Write a new concept or idea on the board and read it aloud. Ask for a volunteer to read aloud what was just written. But instead of moving on to another concept or example, ask for a second volunteer to read aloud the same information. Continue so that each student who feels comfortable can choose to read the information aloud. Students who are at beginning levels of English proficiency will be more comfortable repeating information after they have heard it spoken by their classmates. Note that so students are hearing the same input over and over from other students rather than from the teacher, they will hear other pronunciations, inflections, and intonations.

The activity is very effective for teaching, practicing, and reinforcing concepts such as place value and reading large numbers, and for helping students remember important definitions and vocabulary. For example, English learners need to learn the words million, thousand, hundred, and tens and ones in order to read the number 182,672,824. Teach students to identify numbers in sets of three:

182 (one hundred and eighty two *million*)

672 (six hundred seventy two *thousand*)

824 (eight *hundred* twenty four)

Boost confidence by showing students that if they know their numbers from 1-999 they can read any number simply by grouping them together in threes, and adding the label million, thousand, or hundred. Remember that students may already know these concepts from their native language schooling experiences. These students will only need to learn the English counterparts for the place value vocabulary. Repetition will enable them to learn the words more quickly.

SIOP® Connection

Content Objective:

Students will be able to (SWBAT) . . .

- Read large numbers in math using correct order and number terms.

SIOP® Connection *(continued)*

Language Objectives:

Students will be able to (SWBAT) . . .

- Listen to the teacher and students giving responses, and repeat what they have heard.
- Use the language of place value, including million, thousand, hundred.

Framed Outlines

SIOP® COMPONENT: Comprehensible Input

Grade Levels: 2–12
Subject Areas: All
Grouping Configuration: Small group or whole class
Approximate Time Involved: Depends on text or lesson
Materials: Outline of lesson content with key information excluded

Description:

Create an outline of a text or lesson content leaving out some key information. Students complete the outline as they read the text, listen to a mini-lecture, watch a video, and/or participate in the lesson in some other way. English learners can refer to the framed outline during subsequent lessons and activities.

Framed Outlines are an effective way to provide differentiated instruction. Some students may not need a partially completed outline or organizer; they may create their own independently; others may need more support than the partially completed outline. Provide this by leaving the first letters of key vocabulary and concepts on the outline, and by including icons or simple illustrations as clues. The teacher can also work with a small group of students as they read through the text, completing the Framed Outline together.

SIOP® Connection

Content Objective:

Students will be able to (SWBAT) . . .

- Take notes on a framed outline during (a mini-lecture, text reading, or video viewing).

Language Objectives:

Students will be able to (SWBAT) . . .

- Make meaningful guesses about (missing words or key concepts) in a framed outline.
- Determine if (the guessed words or key concepts) makes sense in the sequence of a framed outline.

The SIOP® Model: Comprehensible Input

Lesson Plans

The following lesson plans (see Figures 4.2–4.3) include the activity "Idiom Match-Up" (p. 57). While the lessons incorporate all of the eight SIOP® components, the emphasis is on Comprehensible Input. Note in the lesson plans that the teacher is very explicit about how students are to complete the tasks, and they are given several opportunities to demonstrate their understanding of idiomatic expressions. Idioms are very challenging for nearly all students, but especially for English learners. The teacher, therefore, can help by using modeling, visuals, and hands-on techniques to make the connection between the idioms and their meanings. Keep in mind that these lesson plans serve as examples. Depending on the grade level you are teaching, and state standards, appropriate resources (websites and content standards) can be substituted to match your students' needs.

FIGURE 4.2 *Elementary Lesson Plan for Comprehensive Input*

Key: SW = Students will; TW = Teacher will; SWBAT = Students will be able to . . . ; HOTS = Higher Order Thinking Skills

---

SIOP® Lesson: Idioms   *Grade: 4*

Content Standard: Strand 1: Reading Process
Concept 4: Vocabulary
Identify figurative language including similes, personification and idioms

Key Vocabulary: idiom, literal & actual
HOTS:
   When might we use idioms to communicate? Why?
   Why would idioms be confusing for someone who does not speak English as a first language?
	Visuals/ Resources:
	Match-up cards, Scholastic Dictionary of Idioms
	www.idiomsite.com
	www.eslcafe.com/idioms/

Connections to Prior Knowledge/ Building Background:
TW ask students: What does it mean "to call it a day?" Think about it, turn to a partner, and share your thoughts.

Content Objectives:	**Meaningful Activities:**	**Review/Assessment:**
1. SWBAT demonstrate knowledge of idioms by defining idioms and their literal meanings.	**1.1** TW share with students some examples of idiomatic expressions: *Give someone a hand* *Call it a day* *Pull someone's leg*	
	1.2 SW do a quick-write, defining what they think the expression means. SW then turn to partners and share their quick-writes.	**1.2** Quick-write definitions
	1.3 TW then define for students what is meant by an idiom/idiomatic expression, present the literal meanings they were asked to define and give an example of how they are used in everyday language including a visual representation from the above website.	

(continued)

FIGURE 4.2 *Elementary Lesson Plan for Comprehensible Input* *(continued)*

Language Objective:		
1. SWBAT demonstrate comprehension of idioms by illustrating the literal meaning of idioms/ and or idiomatic expressions in a "Match–up" activity.	**1.1** SW be asked to come up with a visual representation of one of the idiomatic expressions defined by the teacher.	
	1.2 SW then in groups of 4, take one of the idiomatic expressions they defined in their quick-writes and come up with an illustration for each.	**1.2** Student Illustrations
	1.3 SW post illustrations and meanings around the room.	
	1.4 TW randomly hand out note cards with phrases that interpret how or what the idiomatic expression might be used for in language.	
	1.5 SW in a "Match-up" activity stick the note cards on the appropriate illustration.	**1.5** Students match the (definition, illustration & phrase) to the idiomatic expression.

Wrap-up: Stand up–Sit down
TW read a phrase
SW stand if they believe it is an idiomatic expression
SW stay seated if they do not believe it is an idiomatic expression
SW turn to a partner and share why or why not

Source: Lesson plan created by Melissa Castillo and Nicole Teyechea. Lesson plan content by Melissa Castillo.

FIGURE 4.3 *Secondary Lesson Plan for Comprehensible Input*

Key: SW = Students will; TW = Teacher will; SWBAT = Students will be able to . . . ; HOTS = Higher Order Thinking Skills

SIOP® Lesson : Idiomatic Expressions   *Grade:* 9

> *Content Standard:* Determine the meaning of figurative language, including similes, metaphors, personification, idioms, hyperbole, and technical language.

Key Vocabulary: Expression, literal, Context & Idiom **HOTS:**	**Visuals/Resources:** Barron's Dictionary of American **Idioms,** Scholastic Dictionary of Idioms, computers (1 per group)
When are idioms to communicate? Why? How would you explain to someone what an idiomatic expression is?	www.idiomsite.com www.eslcafe.com/idioms/

Connections to Prior Knowledge/Building Background Information:
TW tell students: *I really want to chill out?* What will I have to do? What would you do? Think about it,
   Turn to a partner and share your thoughts.

FIGURE 4.3 *Secondary Lesson Plan for Comprehensible Input* *(continued)*

Content Objectives:	Meaningful Activities:	Review/Assessment:
1. SWBAT demonstrate application of idioms by identifying idioms and their meanings in a match-up activity.	**1.1** TW share with students examples of idiomatic expressions, for example: *Give someone a hand.* *Call it a day.* *Get out of my hair!* *He's out of his element.*	
	1.2 SW turn to a partner and share what they believe the meaning of each might be. **1.3** TW share one expression, provide its literal meaning and a visual (illustration) representation.	
	1.4 SW then be divided into two groups. One group will be given note cards with idiomatic expressions and illustrations Second group will be given note cards with literal meanings.	**1.4** Student match-up activity (expression & meaning)
	1.5 SW mingle around the room sharing their note cards until they find their "Match-up." SW in pairs share their match with the whole group.	
Language Objectives:		
1. SWBAT demonstrate synthesis of idioms by creating a slideshow defining idioms, including illustrations and how they are used in everyday language.	**1.1** TW translate one of the idiomatic expressions shared earlier to everyday language in context. For example: **Out of your hair:** *I'm sorry to keep interrupting you. I promise I'll be out of your hair in a minute.*	
	1.2 SW in groups of 4 take their idiomatic expressions and create a PowerPoint presentation including a visual representation of the expression and how it translates to everyday language in context.	**1.2** PowerPoint presentation of two idioms, their literal meaning, and translation of how they are used.
	1.3 SW present to the group.	

Wrap-up: Outcome sentences
I learned . . .
I wonder . . .
I thought . . .

Source: Lesson plan created by Melissa Castillo and Nicole Teyechea. Lesson plan content by Melissa Castillo.

chapter 5

Strategies

Overview of the Strategies Component

English learners in the past were often misplaced in remedial and/or special education classes because their lack of English proficiency prevented them from demonstrating content knowledge and literacy skills. At this time, the prevailing thought was also that academic instruction was not possible until ELs had reached at least an intermediate level of fluency in English.

Today we know that we cannot wait until students develop English proficiency to teach them grade-level content information. They can and will learn, given appropriate instruction, support and assistance. We need to recognize that as students learn English, they must also develop strategies to critically analyze and effectively learn.

The Strategies component focuses on the cognitive and metacognitive strategies that learners use to make sense of new information and concepts. Examples of learning strategies include rereading, note-taking, organizing information, predicting, self-questioning, evaluating, monitoring, clarifying, and summarizing. Studies have shown that explicit teaching and modeling of these (and other) strategies helps students become more strategic in their thinking and learning. Teachers can further develop students' strategic thinking by planning and asking higher-order questions and requiring tasks that promote critical thinking. It is no longer acceptable to ask English learners a preponderance of low-level questions.

There are many ways teachers can provide scaffolding support that is gradually released as students begin to independently apply their new knowledge. Examples of instructional scaffolding include the appropriate use of graphic organizers, partner- and small-group instruction and practice, adapted texts, partially completed outlines, and texts with key concepts and vocabulary marked with a highlighter. Verbal scaffolding includes techniques such as think-alouds, paraphrasing, repetition, careful enunciation, and frequent review of contextualized vocabulary. We have often heard from teachers that the entire SIOP® Model is about scaffolding instruction for English learners; we agree.

The Strategies component includes the following features:

13. Ample opportunities provided for students to use learning strategies.

14. Scaffolding techniques consistently used, assisting and supporting student understanding (e.g., think-alouds).

15. A variety of questions or tasks that promote higher-order thinking skills (e.g., literal, analytical, and interpretive questions).

Ideas and Activities for Teaching Strategies

Directed Reading-Thinking Activity (DR-TA)

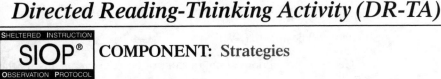

COMPONENT: Strategies

(Adapted from Stauffer, 1969)

Grade Levels: All (for K–1, this can be a Directed Listening-Thinking Activity, when the teacher does a read-aloud, a DL-TA)

Subject Areas: Language Arts (or any subject area when a piece of fiction is used)

Grouping Configuration: Whole class

Approximate Time Involved: Depends on the length of the text

Materials: Rich, narrative text; DR-TA is most effective with short stories that have a "cliff-hanger" ending

Description:

For more than 30 years teachers have used the DR-TA to assist students in learning about how to strategically comprehend narrative (fiction) text. The teacher and students stop periodically throughout the reading of a story or book to contemplate predictions about what might follow logically in the next section of the text.

Begin the lesson with a question about what the class members think the story or book will be about, based on its title. As students respond, use a variety of probes, such as:

- "With a title like . . . . , what do you think this story will be about?"
- "Let's read to find out."
- Revisit predictions: "Did . . . . happen? If not, why not?"
- "What do you think is going to happen next? What makes you think so?"
- "Where did you get that idea?"
- "What made you think that?"
- "Tell me more about that . . ."

It is important for the class to revisit previously made predictions after sections of text are read; students will then come to understand how predictions (and their confirmation or disconfirmation) impacts comprehension. As the students focus their thinking on character (and author) motivations, the problems characters face and the reasons for their behavior, students can "vote" on which predictions are most likely and explain why as the plot unfolds. Note that DR-TA is also effective for longer novels, using chapter-to-chapter discussions that focus on what students think will happen, what really happens, and why.

SIOP® Connection

Content Objective:

Students will be able to (SWBAT) . . .

- Generate predictions about (a story or book's) events, justify their predictions, and after reading, confirm or disconfirm their predictions.

Language Objective:

Students will be able to (SWBAT) . . .

- Use the following sentence frames when making predictions, justifying predictions, and confirming or disconfirming predictions:

  "I predict that _____ will happen, because _____."

  "I wish to change my prediction to _____ because

  _____."

  "My prediction was confirmed when _____."

  "My prediction was disconfirmed when _____."

SQP2RS ("Squeepers")

SIOP® SHELTERED INSTRUCTION OBSERVATION PROTOCOL **COMPONENT:** Strategies

(Echevarria, Vogt, & Short, 2008; Vogt, 2000)

Grade Levels: All (K–1 teachers use informational big books; upper grade teachers use informational or expository texts)

Subject Areas: Science, Social Studies, Language Arts; any subjects where students are reading informational and expository texts

Grouping Configurations: Whole class, small groups, partners, with individual accountability

Approximate Time Involved: Depends on the length of the text and age/reading ability of students

Materials: Informational or expository text

Description:

SQP2RS ("Squeepers") is an instructional framework for teaching content information to all students, including those needing modifications. It reinforces the major metacognitive strategies that highly proficient readers use: predicting, self-questioning, monitoring/clarifying, evaluating, summarizing/synthesizing (Dole, Duffy, Roehler, & Pearson, 1991). These strategies reflect the ways effective readers think about text; when we teach and regularly reinforce them students become more strategic in their thinking. The six steps to the SQP2RS/Squeepers instructional framework are:

1. *Survey:* This step helps students activate and use their background knowledge and experience related to the topic of study, and "sets the stage" for what students will be reading about in a piece of expository text. Teach students to survey an assigned section of text by modeling your own thinking processes with a think-aloud. Make a transparency of the text students will read and model how you would survey the text: "I see there are bold-print headings, so I know this is key information that will help me know what the big ideas will be. I also see some bolded sub-headings and italic words; I know this means they are important concepts and vocabulary. I see a photograph here that illustrates a major idea . . . . (etc.)"

2. *Question:* During this step students (in partners or small groups) formulate questions about the text they have just surveyed. Use the following prompt to engage them in this process: "Based on your survey, think of two or three questions that you think will be answered by reading this text. You probably can't answer the questions now, but with more information you will be able to do so." (If you teach K–1, you'll need to assist students in wording the questions in the beginning.) As students orally share their questions, record them on the Squeepers Chart (see Figure 5.1), and indicate with asterisks/stars how many groups or pairs have generated the same or similar questions. Several questions will emerge during this process that are deemed "important," because more than one group came up with them.

3. *Predicting:* This step builds upon the questions generated previously, helping students determine what they think will be the most important concepts in the article or chapter

Questions: *We will find answers to...*	Predictions: *We will learn...*

FIGURE 5.1 *SQP2RS Chart*

to be read. Not coincidentally, determining the major concepts and ideas is the most challenging part of reading expository text. Your job is to help students narrow their focus, using the questions (especially those marked with asterisks/stars) to predict four or five key concepts students think they will be learning. The predictions may restate some of the questions: Predicting and questioning are integrated thinking processes; it is expected that there will be a relationship between them. If students use the lesson's content and language objectives to help them generate predictions, so much the better!

Note that the first three steps of Squeepers (Survey, Question, Predict) should only take about 5–7 minutes once students have learned the process.

4. *Reading:* In the beginning have students read the selection with partners or in small groups. This provides scaffolded support for students who need it, and ensures that students finish reading at about the same time. Eventually, you may wish to let students choose how they will read the text: independently or with others. While reading, students should note places in the text where they have found answers to the questions initially asked—and where predictions were confirmed. Encourage students to use sticky notes or tabs, or highlighter tape to mark their texts (they can highlight, underline, and write directly on duplicated texts). This interaction with the text is very important; you're teaching students to do what accomplished readers do when they read challenging texts.

5. *Respond:* During the response stage, students discuss together (in whole class or small groups) the answers to the questions posed earlier and the predictions that were confirmed or disconfirmed (avoid using the terms "right" and "wrong" when discussing predictions). It is important to discuss any questions not answered in the text, to contemplate which questions were answered, which were not, and why: "Might we find answers to some of the questions in the next section? In another chapter? Did the author take us in a different direction than we originally thought? Are there other questions we should be asking before we read more? Are there any questions we should eliminate?" The response step is intended to be a time of discussion, reflection, and interaction, not a time for students to write answers to the generated questions.

6. *Summarize:* At this point, all students should be able to summarize the key content concepts that were introduced and discussed in the text. The length and complexity of the summary, and whether it is stated orally or in writing, depends on students' language proficiencies and grade level. It is reasonable to expect a few sentences from everyone (or perhaps a drawing for a beginning English speaker). If you have students who need modifications, write key vocabulary on the board to help them incorporate these words into their summaries. Model the summarizing process so that you don't receive a "retelling" rather than a summary.

Once students have learned the entire SQP2RS sequence, revisit it every week or so, remembering that its purpose is to teach students to effectively read expository chapters and articles, while they develop cognitive and metacognitive strategies.

SIOP® Connection

Content Objectives:

(for a lesson on Egyptian mummies) students will be able to (SWBAT) . . .

- Explain the importance of the mummification process in relation to Egyptian culture.
- Explain the mummification process.
- Show on a map where mummies have been found.

Language Objectives:

Students will be able to (SWBAT) . . .

- Talk about a mummy, using descriptive adjectives.
- Compare the following words according to their word class and meaning: mummy, mummification, mummified.
- Ask questions about the text they read.

Questioning Prompts for Different Levels of Language Acquisition

SIOP® SHELTERED INSTRUCTION OBSERVATION PROTOCOL **COMPONENT:** Strategies

(Adapted from Long Beach Unified School District)

Grade Levels: All
Subject Areas: All
Grouping Configuration: Individual, partners, small group, whole class
Approximate Time Involved: On-going process in every lesson
Materials: None

Description:

Teachers will vary their questioning prompts based on the different levels of language acquisition represented in their classrooms. The following prompts elicit responses that are sensitive to students' English proficiency levels. Remember that students at lower levels of language proficiency are not necessarily at lower levels of cognitive ability; they may be able to use higher level thinking skills in their primary language but have a difficult time understanding academic content and expressing their knowledge in English.

It takes practice to craft higher level questions and tasks that allow students to use whatever language skills they have to participate in appropriate grade level activities. The following suggestions can help teachers see how students' responses can become more complex as they gain additional English proficiency. When activities vary from literal to interpretative to applied, teachers can create heterogeneous groups with students of different English proficiency levels. These groupings provide appropriate and necessary scaffolding for students who are beginning English speakers.

- Beginning Pre-Production: Ask students to point to something or touch the answer, or signal by clapping or physically moving items in a lesson.
- Beginning Early Production: Ask questions that require a yes/no, either/or, or one- or two-word answer.
- Beginning Early Speech Emergence: Students can respond in simple sentences. Ask questions such as, "Which animal was your favorite in the story? Why?"
- Early Intermediate: Students can generate and respond in simple sentences. Ask questions such as, "Tell me about your story" or "What did you do to solve that problem?"
- Intermediate: Students can generate and respond in simple connected narratives. They can answer questions such as, "What happened in the story?" and "How will the story end?"
- Early Advanced: Students can respond in sequential narrative, justify, summarize, evaluate, and synthesize information, compare items and answer "why" questions.
- Advanced: Students with near native speech fluency can be asked to explain cycles and processes in detail.

SIOP® Connection

Content Objectives:

Students will be able to (SWBAT) . . .

- Identify three key concepts about (topic) by participating in a question/answer activity.

Language Objective:

Students will be able to (SWBAT) . . .

- Use gestures, words, phrases, and sentences to answer questions about (topic).

Canned Questions

SIOP® | **COMPONENT:** Strategies
SHELTERED INSTRUCTION
OBSERVATION PROTOCOL

(Adapted from Karen Mettler, Prescott Senior Elementary School, Modesto, CA)

Grade Levels: 2–12
Subject Areas: All
Grouping Configuration: Whole class
Approximate Time Involved: 20 minutes
Materials: Coffee can with hole cut in lid; question strips

Description:

Write (on strips of paper) a variety of questions related to the particular topic being studied. The questions should range from lower to higher levels of thinking. Ask students to demonstrate (according to Bloom's Taxonomy):

- Knowledge by defining, locating, underlining, labeling or identifying.
- Comprehension by describing, summarizing, explaining, or paraphrasing.
- Application by computing, building, or giving an example.
- Analysis by categorizing, classifying, comparing and contrasting.
- Synthesis by combining, creating, designing, or predicting.
- Evaluation by concluding, defining, justifying and prioritizing.

Place the question strips in a can. Group students as partners or in small groups (to lower anxiety and to scaffold). The teacher draws out the questions, one by one, and students work together to answer them. Occasionally the teacher may pull a question and based on its difficulty (i.e. the English proficiency required for response), select individual students to answer. When this is done, all students gain exposure to questions of varied cognitive levels, even though they are only responsible for answering the questions that are appropriate for their level of English proficiency.

Students may also (individually or in groups) submit questions to the Question Can. These can be drawn for other students to answer. Teachers can teach students how to ask higher order questions using QAR's: Question-Answer-Relationships (p. 79).

SIOP® Connection

Content Objective:

Students will be able to (SWBAT) . . .

- Respond to questions written at various cognitive levels on (a topic).

(continued)

SIOP® Connection *(continued)*

Language Objectives:

Students will be able to (SWBAT) . . .

- Display their knowledge of (topic) by using complete sentences when answering a question.

- Answer questions on increasingly sophisticated levels of cognition using the following prompts:

    Knowledge: The definition of (topic) is _____.

    Comprehension: (Topic) can be explained as _____.

    Application: An example of (topic) is _____.

    Analysis: (Topic) can be compared to _____.

    Synthesis: If I create a diagram of (topic) I would include _____ in my diagram.

    Evaluation: We can conclude that (topic) _____.

Question-Answer Relationships (QAR)

SIOP® | **COMPONENT:** Strategies

(Raphael, 1984)

Grade Levels: K–12 (K–2 use two levels: On the Page; In My Head)
Subject Areas: All
Grouping Configuration: Small group, whole class
Approximate Time Involved: In the beginning teaching QAR takes time, patience, and practice; eventually, students should be able to identify the types of questions rather quickly.
Materials: Narrative or expository texts and a list of questions

Description:

The National Reading Panel (NRP) (2000) reported a relationship between teaching students how to answer questions, and higher levels of comprehension. The Panel reported further that teaching students how to ask questions positively affects comprehension and this activity, QAR, does both. Students learn to determine the type of questions they are being asked, and how to ask questions at varying levels.

It is important to teach and to model QAR. Begin by explaining that when students are answering questions about a text, the answers may be found "In the Book" or "In My Head." Within these two categories are four types of questions:

In the Book

- *Right There:* "Right There" questions require the reader to go back into the text to find specific information for the answer. Often labeled as literal, "Right There" questions may include words or phrases like: "According to the passage . . . ;" "How many . . . . ?" "Who is . . . . ?" "Where is . . . . ?" "What is . . . . ?"

- *Think and Search:* "Think and Search" questions require the reader to think about the relationships among the ideas and/or information discussed in a text. Readers are asked to look back at a passage and think about how the information or ideas fit together. "Think and Search" questions can include the words, "The main idea of the passage was . . . . ," "Compare and contrast . . . ," "What is the relationship between . . . ?"

In My Head

- *Author and Me:* "Author and Me" questions require the reader to use prior knowledge and experience in addition to information from the text. The answer is not directly stated, but inferred. These questions ask the reader to formulate ideas and opinions based upon what is in a passage. "Author and Me" questions sometimes include phrases such as "The author implies . . ." and "The passage suggests . . ."

- *On My Own:* The answer to an "On My Own" question isn't stated explicitly or inferentially, but requires readers to use their own background experiences and knowledge. "On My Own" questions may include phrases such as, "In your opinion . . . ," "Based on your experience . . . ," and "Think about someone or something you know . . ."

FIGURE 5.2 *QAR Poster*
Source: Sarah Russell.

For children in grades K–2, it might be more realistic to introduce two types of questions: "On the Page" and "In My Head." As children become more proficient English readers (and/or speakers), the four question types can be presented. For older students, when they are answering end-of-chapter questions or completing a study guide, suggest that they not only provide an answer to the questions, but write what type of question they are answering. (See Figure 5.2 for QAR posters designed by Sarah Russell, ESL teacher, Washoe County School District).

Anticipation/Reaction Guide

 **COMPONENT:** Strategies

(Readence, Bean & Baldwin, 2004)

Grade Levels: 2–12

Subject Areas: All

Grouping Configuration: Small groups, whole class

Approximate Time Involved: Approximately 10 minutes before lesson and 10 minutes after to discuss students' responses

Materials: An anticipation/reaction guide and text to read

Description:

Create agree/disagree or true/false statements based on the text and/or content concepts to be studied. Before reading, students individually read through the statements and mark their responses on the left side (Anticipation) of the guide. Students then share responses with a partner and make predictions about what they will be learning, which sets their purpose for reading. After reading the text, students mark their responses to the same statements on the right side of the guide (Reaction). The class then discusses how the text reading changed some of their responses. Anticipation/Reaction Guides can also be used to preview and review information on a unit that will be or has been studied. For very young children or beginning speakers of English, simple illustrations can support the reading of the guide statements.

Topic: Natural Disasters Agree (A) or Disagree (D)

Anticipation   Reaction

Hurricanes cause the most damage of any type of natural disaster in the United States.

Insurance companies should not be held responsible for covering damage to homes and businesses from natural disasters..

People should be able to rebuild their homes in the same places even though the location is commonly in the path of hurricanes..

The U.S. Government must refit all buildings and highways that are earthquake-prone.

SIOP® Connection

Content Objectives:

Students will be able to (SWBAT) . . .

- Agree or disagree about Anticipation statements written about (a topic).
- Make predictions about what they will learn by reading about (a topic).

SIOP® Connection *(continued)*

- Review after reading, their earlier predictions and clarify questions or misconceptions about (a topic).

Language Objective:

Students will be able to (SWBAT) . . .

- Confirm or disconfirm predictions, using the following sentence frames:

  "I think this is true because _____."

  "I think this is false because _____."

  "I confirmed my prediction when I read _____."

  "I disconfirmed my prediction when I read _____."

  "I agree with the statement because _____."

  "I disagree with the statement because _____."

Progressive Maps

SIOP® COMPONENT: Strategies

(Adapted from Shelly Frei, Long Beach Unified School District)

Grade Levels: All
Subject Areas: History and social studies (also other subjects)
Grouping Configuration: Small groups, whole class
Approximate Time Involved: Ongoing process
Materials: Chart paper and markers

Description:

Progressive Maps encourage students to visually organize old and new information. A unit begins with a directed drawing on a map (the chart paper).

For example, for a unit on Native Americans, students might add grass and streams to an empty map, indicating that no one has lived there yet, adding various landforms (desert, forest, mountain range). New information is added to their maps (or map, if it is a whole class activity) as students learn more. A picture of the buffalo that came from the north can be added, as well as drawings of the people that followed. Markers or labels can be used to indicate where various tribes settled.

These same maps are brought out again as the class begins to study the westward movement of the European settlers in the United States. The information on Native Americans is already on the map; students can now add the exploration ships, the new colonies, and the covered wagons that traveled near Native American settlements. As the map goes through changes, students receive visual support to develop higher thinking skills as they evaluate changes, hypothesize possible cause and effect situations, and defend opinions about what happened and why. When a timeline and labels are added to the map, students connect the visual representations to the key vocabulary and concepts.

SIOP® Connection

Content Objective:

Students will be able to (SWBAT) . . .

- Visually represent their knowledge of (a topic) by creating drawings on a Progressive Map.

Language Objectives:

Students will be able to (SWBAT) . . .

- Describe what that they have visualized about (a topic) through the use of key phrases, including:

SIOP® Connection (continued)

"In my head I see _____."

"I picture _____ because _____."

"I visualize _____ because _____."

- Use sequence words that represent time:

"In the fifteenth century, _____."

"What followed was _____."

"But today, _____."

"In the future, _____."

T-Chart Graphic Organizer

SIOP® SHELTERED INSTRUCTION OBSERVATION PROTOCOL **COMPONENT:** Strategies

Grade Levels: All (teacher records information for lower grades)
Subject Areas: All
Grouping Configuration: Individual, partners, small groups, whole class brainstorming
Materials: Chart paper for whole class T-Chart, or T-Charts for students to complete individually

Description:

A T-Chart is a graphic organizer to help students classify information (see Figure 5.3). First, model the process by drawing a large T-Chart on chart paper; write on the T-Chart while the class brainstorms information about a topic. Then ask partners to fill out a T-Chart to classify the previously brainstormed information. A teacher can further scaffold this activity by providing students with information that is then classified into two lists. Eventually, the students are asked to generate their own items for the T-Chart. A triple T-Chart (sometimes called an M-Chart) allows for three categories.

For example, the general topic is Animals and the two categories are Wild Animals and Domesticated Animals (or animals that are pets). Students brainstorm examples and explain their rationale for placing each animal in the appropriate category.

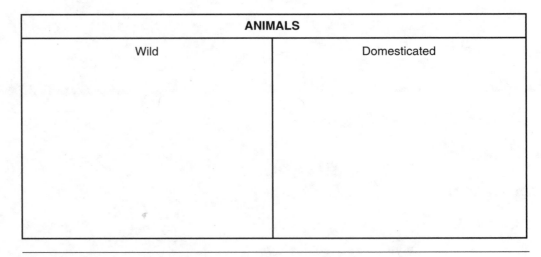

ANIMALS	
Wild	Domesticated

FIGURE 5.3 *T-Chart Graphic Organizer*

SIOP® Connection

Content Objectives:

Students will be able to (SWBAT) . . .

- Brainstorm what they know about (a topic).
- Classify their ideas about (a topic) on a T-Chart.
- Explain their rationale for classifying information about (a topic) in a particular category.

Language Objective:

Students will be able to (SWBAT) . . .

- Use classifying language when determining which examples belong to each category, and justify the reasons for their classification, using sentence frames such as:

  "I think _____ belongs to this group because

  _____."

  "I am not sure which group this _____ belongs in because

  _____."

Split Page Note Taking

SIOP® SHELTERED INSTRUCTION OBSERVATION PROTOCOL

COMPONENT: Strategies

Grade Levels: 3–12
Subject Areas: All
Grouping Configuration: Small groups, whole class
Approximate Time Involved: Depends on text length and difficulty
Materials: Binder paper

Description:

Before the lesson begins, students divide a piece of paper in half. On the left side of the paper, direct them to write down a few questions about the topic. As the class reads through the text (individually, in partners, or in a group), each student writes notes to answer the questions on the right side of the paper. After practicing this technique several times, students can be taught to write their own questions by previewing the text, and/or using the headings by turning them into questions. After much modeling of the activity, students will be able to independently create the questions.

It is helpful to teach students (especially English learners) the following:

- A "who question" indicates that the answer will include a person's name.
- A "what question" indicates that the answer will include a description of an action.
- A "when question" indicates that the answer will include a time frame for something happening.
- A "where question" indicates that the answer will include a place where something happened.
- A "why question" indicates that the answer will include an explanation of a person's actions.
- A "how question" indicates that the answer will include a description of a process.

When students have completed a Split Page Note Taking activity for an article or chapter, the notes/answers they have written on the right side of the paper can be used as a foundation for summary writing and for reviewing the material prior to a quiz or test. Keep in mind that students who have learned to ask and answer questions in their native language need to learn the corresponding English vocabulary. Students who have not developed literacy in their native language will need more explicit instruction and modeling of asking and answering questions.

🔧 SIOP® Connection

Content Objective:

Students will be able to (SWBAT) . . .

- Identify five benefits of universal health care for people in poverty after reading an opinion-piece. (Notice how this content objective relates to the actual content of the

SIOP® Connection *(continued)*

article students will read. The Split Page Note Taking activity is the "means to the end," not the "end".)

Language Objective:

Students will be able to (SWBAT) . . .

- Read an article and identify information based on key words in questions: *who, what, when, where, why*.

Stop and Think

 **COMPONENT: Strategies**

(Adapted from Shelly Frei, Long Beach Unified School District)

Grade Levels: Developing readers (of varying ages)
Subject Areas: All
Grouping Configuration: Individual, small groups, whole class
Approximate Time Involved: 5 minutes
Materials: Narrative or expository text

Description:

As they read through a short passage in a text, proficient readers accomplish many tasks; make predictions, infer information, visualize a scene, and generate questions. They usually do these tasks without even realizing they are doing them. But beginning readers often don't realize that they are supposed to do this, in part because they are focusing on decoding words. These students may be confused after reading when their classmates can answer questions and they can't because they're not comprehending. As teachers, we tell our struggling readers to re-read, but they often do so with the same results.

There are a number of ways to scaffold skills and strategies for beginning and developing readers. First, be aware of all that you do "in an instant" of reading; explicitly explain the skills and strategies good readers use. During read-alouds, model your reading processes one at a time in a think-aloud, such as, "When I read this, I think of . . ." During shared and guided reading, give a hand signal (like placing a finger to the side of the head) or sound signal that tells students to "stop and think." During this time they are to stop reading, practice the skill or strategy they are learning that day, share their thinking with a partner, and then continue reading. Explicitly teach thinking strategies such as: *imagine, remember, think of a question, predict, pretend, recall, listen, look, think about, visualize, solve mentally, summarize to yourself,* or *make an inference* (or *infer*). Model what you mean by each of these terms; think-alouds provide a great mental model for students. They'll learn what you do when you engage in these varied thinking and reading strategies.

SIOP® Connection

Content Objectives:

Students will be able to (SWBAT) . . .

- Make personal connections during the reading of (a text) as they practice the "Stop and Think" strategy.
- Use the signal of placing a finger to the side of their head to demonstrate that they are taking the time to "Stop and Think."

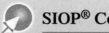 **SIOP® Connection** *(continued)*

Language Objective:

Students will be able to (SWBAT) . . .

- Articulate how they are making connections to what they know and what they have experienced, using the following sentence frames:

  "When I read _____ it made me remember when

  _____."

  "This part of the story/article/chapter makes me think of a time when

  _____."

You Are the Teacher!

SIOP® | **COMPONENT:** Strategies

Grade Levels: 3–12
Subject Areas: All
Grouping Configuration: Small groups within whole class setting
Approximate Time Involved: 45–60 minutes
Materials: Chart paper and informational text

Description:

Students need explicit instruction for this activity in how to move around the classroom appropriately. "You are the Teacher!" encourages students to learn important information by teaching it to other class members. After reading and/or researching a selection of text, in small groups students create a chart or poster, using words, illustrations, or a graphic organizer to arrange the information learned. The posters are then attached to the walls around the classroom.

Members within each group decide who will remain at their poster to teach the next group, and who will move on to a spot in front of the next poster. Students choose a number from 1–100, do "Rock/Paper/Scissors," or use colored strips selected from an envelope (one color stays; the other moves on). Beginning English speakers should be paired with more fluent speakers, whether they stay or move on.

Those students going to the next poster move in a clockwise rotation; the students who remain with the poster then teach the rotated students about the information on the chart or poster. At each rotation, students again decide who stays and who rotates. Eventually students will end up back at their original posters. It is important that each final group report the key information from their poster to the class so that the "playing telephone" effect is minimized. While it is helpful for students to have an opportunity to share information and interact with each other, it is critical that the content information be correctly "taught" by the students.

SIOP® Connection

Content Objectives:

Students will be able to (SWBAT) . . .

- Create posters containing pictures and information about (a topic).
- Share with fellow students the information they have learned about (a topic).

Language Objective:

Students will be able to (SWBAT) . . .

- Clarify what is being taught to them, what they understand and what they don't understand as they move from group to group, using the following sentence frames:

SIOP® Connection *(continued)*

"I understand that this is about _____."

"I don't understand _____."

"I have a question about _____."

"Can you explain _____ to me again?"

Value Line

SIOP® COMPONENT: Strategies (and Interaction)

(Temple, 1998; Vogt, 2000)

Grade Levels: All
Subject Areas: All
Grouping Configuration: Small groups, whole class
Approximate Time Involved: 15 minutes
Materials: None

Description:

A Value Line requires that students apply knowledge they have just learned, draw on past learning and experiences, and take a position (i.e., state their values) about difficult topics. High school students might study a piece of pending legislation intended to establish a parent's right to know over a teenager's right to privacy. After reading and discussing the legislation, two students "in character" serve as advocates for each position, urging class members to take one of the advocated positions (parents' rights/students' rights). The mock debate (ends of the Value Line) incorporates clear arguments and specific support for the respective viewpoints.

When the advocates finish arguing their position, the other students take a position on the spectrum; one end of the Value Line represents the parents' right to know and the other represents the students' privacy rights. Before they assume their place on the spectrum (an imaginary line that bisects the classroom), students negotiate with those around them to determine where they belong on the line. While doing this, the students also attempt to persuade their class members to move toward one position or the other. At the end of the exercise class members articulate why they chose a particular spot and what perspectives on the topic people standing to their left or the right held.

Value Line can be modified by having students assume an identity other than their own (such as historical figures or literary characters); students then take a stand on the line about a topic or event relevant to their character. All students assume a character's identity as they take a stand, defend their positions, and try to persuade other characters to move toward one end or the other. For example, in the classic story "The Lottery" by Shirley Jackson (1982), the ends of the line would represent "yes" or "no" positions in answer to the question: "Should the town's annual lottery continue?" Students assume the role of the townspeople arguing for one position or the other until everyone has taken a stand.

Younger students can be involved in this same activity using stories, and the decisions and choices characters must make. Questions such as, "What do you think you would do?" or "What do you think Ramona should do?" can be used to coach students. They can then begin to see how their own choices might be similar to or different from those of their favorite characters in picture books.

Some teachers believe that English learners cannot participate in an activity such as Value Line. While ELs may need scaffolding to understand the content concepts, as good thinkers they can certainly "take their stand" along the line and with a partner, to explain why they have assumed their stance.

SIOP® Connection

Content Objective:

Students will be able to (SWBAT) . . .

- Demonstrate their knowledge and understanding of (topic) by assuming a place along a continuum of perspectives (the Value Line).

Language Objectives:

Students will be able to (SWBAT) . . .

- Orally explain to students around them why they have assumed the position they have on the Value Line, using the following sentence frame:

  "I am standing here on the Value Line because _____."

- Attempt to convince other students to change their position by using the following sentence frame:

  "I think you should move over here because _____."

Adapted Venn Diagram

COMPONENT: Strategies

Grade Levels: 2–12 (for K–1, teacher can complete the Diagram on chart paper)
Subject Areas: All
Grouping Configuration: Individual, partners, small groups, whole class
Approximate Time Involved: 15 minutes
Materials: Adapted Venn Diagram (see Figure 5.4)

FIGURE 5.4 *Adapted Venn Diagram*

Description:

A Venn Diagram can be used to compare and contrast information. It includes two intersected circles, with information about two different concepts, ideas, or objects written in each circle. Where the circles intersect, students write information about what is the same about the two concepts, ideas, or objects. The adapted Venn Diagram uses intersected squares instead of circles, arranged side by side, with the second square slightly lower, giving more room to write the examples of how the two things are the same. Another adaptation is to use sticky notes, because they are movable and can be shifted around the Venn Diagram when new learning takes place or thinking changes.

SIOP® Connection

Content Objective:

Students will be able to (SWBAT) . . .

- Compare and contrast the work of two authors.

Language Objective:

Students will be able to (SWBAT) . . .

- Use key vocabulary to articulate differences and similarities between the authors (similar, both, different, but)

  "They are similar because they both _____."

  "They are different because _____."

  "_____ writes about _____, but

  _____ writes about _____."

The SIOP® Model: Strategies

Lesson Plans

The following lesson plans include the activity You are the Teacher (p. 92). While the lessons incorporate all eight of the SIOP® components, the emphasis here is on Strategies. Students are given ample opportunities to use learner strategies throughout both lessons. Note the use of metacognitve strategy practice as students ask the question, "Do I understand the material being presented?" The sentence frames assist English learners in formulating questions and checking their own understanding. Students also engage in cognitive strategy practice as they organize information from the text into a poster format and work cooperatively with peers, developing social/affective strategies.

The lessons also provide ample scaffolding for the ELs so they can meet content and language objectives. Rather than simply assigning an essay or response paragraph, the lesson supports learning by allowing students to first work with their peers to understand the characters' attributes. Only then is an independent writing assignment assigned. Finally, the lessons incorporate the use of higher order thinking questions as students evaluate the characters and their roles in the story.

Keep in mind these lesson plans serve as examples. Depending on your grade level and state standard, substitute the appropriate literature selection and content standards. This example is intended to demonstrate how to incorporate the Strategies component of the SIOP® Model into a lesson plan.

FIGURE 5.5 *Elementary Lesson Plan*

Key: SW = Students will; TW = Teacher will; SWBAT = Students will be able to . . . ; HOTS = Higher Order Thinking Skills

SIOP® Lesson: Character Attributes   Grade 3

Content Standard: Concept 5: Literary Response
Literary response is the writer's reaction to a literary selection. The response includes the writer's interpretation, analysis, opinion, and/or feelings about the piece of literature and selected elements within it.
PO 1: Write a reflection to a literature selection (e.g., journal entry, book review).

Key Vocabulary: Character, plot HOTS: Which character would you rather be and why?	Supplementary Materials: poster board, the book *Tops and Bottoms*

Connections to Prior Knowledge/ Building Background:
SW list characteristics of the main characters (Rabbit and Hare) in small groups.
Groups will share one of their characteristics with the whole group.

Content Objectives:	Meaningful Activities:	Review/Assessment:
1. SWBAT describe character attributes by creating a poster of one of the two characters.	**1.1** TW model using a think aloud to create a poster using the character attributes from Goldilocks as an example from the book "Goldilocks and the Three Bears" (Building Background)	

(continued)

FIGURE 5.5 *Elementary Lesson Plan* *(continued)*

	1.2 SW in small groups create a poster for their assigned character illustrating and summarizing the characteristics that they brainstormed in Building Background.	1.2 SW include at least 2-3 characteristics and illustrate one pertinent scene from the book.
Language Objectives:		
1. SWBAT explain in writing their opinions and /or feelings of how their characters' attributes affected the story's outcome.	1.1 SW share their posters with their peers in the "You Are the Teacher" activity. "Teaching Ideas" 1.2 SW as they move through the activity, use the following sentence frames to clarify their own understanding after each poster presentation "I understand that Bear or Hare's _____ affected the story by _____;" " I don't understand _____." "I have a question about _____."	1.1 Teacher observation
2. SWBAT compose a paragraph discussing how Bear and Hare's individual attributes contributed to the story's outcome.	2.1 SW independently write a literary response in their journals explaining how both of the characters individual attributes affected the story's outcome.	2.1 SW include at least two specific examples of how each characters attributes contributed to the story's outcome.

Wrap-up: Oral Sharing with a Partner
Which character would you rather be and why?
SW share their responses with a partner, then with a group of four.

Source: Lesson plan created by Melissa Castillo and Nicole Teyechea. Lesson plan content by Melissa Castillo and Kendra Moreno.

FIGURE 5.6 *Secondary Lesson Plan*

Key: SW = Students will; TW = Teacher will; SWBAT = Students will be able to . . . ; HOTS = Higher Order Thinking Skills

SIOP® Lesson: Character Analysis   Grade 9

Content Standard: Strand 3: Writing Applications
Concept 5: Literary Response
PO 1: Write a literary analysis that describes the author's use of characterization.

Key Vocabulary: characterization, plot **HOTS:** How would you evaluate _____ role in the progression of the plot?	**Supplementary Materials:** poster board, *Of Mice and Men* by John Steinbeck

Connections to Prior Knowledge/Building Background Information:
SW brainstorm characteristics of the main characters (George, Lennie, Curley, Curley's wife and Slim) in small groups.
Groups will share 3 of their characteristics with the whole group.

(continued)

. . . .

99

FIGURE 5.6 *Secondary Lesson Plan*   *(continued)*

Content Objectives:	Meaningful Activities:	Review/Assessment:
1. SWBAT demonstrate synthesis of writing a literary analysis that describes the author's use of characterization by creating a poster of one character, including how he or she moves the plot of the story forward.	**1.1** TW model using a think-aloud how to create a poster using the character "Crooks," depicting how he contributed to the progression of the Plot of *Of Mice and Men*. Example: Lonely, Bitter, Disempowered , Vulnerable *"Perhaps what Crooks wants more than anything else is a sense of belonging—to enjoy simple pleasures such as the right to enter the bunkhouse or to play cards with the other men. This desire would explain why, even though he has reason to doubt George and Lennie's talk about the farm that they want to own, Crooks cannot help but ask if there might be room for him to come along and hoe in the garden."*	
	1.2 SW in small groups create a poster for their assigned character illustrating and summarizing how the characteristics that they brainstormed in Building Background contribute to the plot.	**1.2** SW include at least 3-5 characteristics, SW illustrate one pertinent scene from the novel.
Language Objectives:		
1. SWBAT write a literary analysis that describes the author's use of characterization, by explaining how their chosen character moved the plot of the story forward.	**1.1** SW share their posters with their peers in the "You Are the Teacher" activity.	**1.1** Teacher observation
	1.2 SW use the following sentence frames to clarify their own understanding after each poster presentation: "I understand that _____ contributed by _____." "I don't understand _____." "I have a question about _____."	**1.2** Completed sentence frames
2. SWBAT compose an essay discussing all five characters and their roles in moving the plot forward.	**2.1** SW independently write a literary analysis explaining how each of the characters served to move the plot forward.	**2.1** SW include all five characters and at least two specific examples of how each contributed to the plot; depending on students' language proficiency, the "essay" may consist of • 5–6 sentences • one paragraph • 2–3 paragraphs

Wrap-up: Students in pairs will orally share their essays.

Source: Lesson plan created by Melissa Castillo and Nicole Teyechea. Lesson plan content by Melissa Castillo and Kendra Moreno.

chapter 6

Interaction

Overview of the Interaction Component

One thing we know for certain about English learners is that they will not become proficient speakers of the language unless they have frequent opportunities to use it. While this seems obvious, it's surprising how few chances there are each day for ELs to speak English. English learners are likely to speak their native language before and after school, during breaks, recess, and lunch, if they have peers who speak their same native language. Teachers who monopolize the vast majority of classroom talk, as is common practice, compound the problem and ELs have even fewer opportunities to speak English.

Effective SIOP® teachers incorporate into their lesson plans multiple opportunities for their students to use English, in writing, in reading, and in interaction with the teacher and other students. SIOP® teachers also provide time for students to process in English what they are hearing prior to answering questions or participating in discussion. Students occasionally work independently during SIOP® lessons, but more often they learn with partners and in small groups. The teacher purposely decreases the amount of teacher-talk by planning few lectures (and "mini" ones at that), and by turning the talk over to students with probes such as, "Tell me more about this;" "Why do you think so?" "Where did you get that idea?" "Will you explain your thinking to your partner?" When an English learner has difficulty understanding a direction or concept in English, the teacher encourages clarification in the student's language, if possible, by another student, an instructional assistant, or by the teacher. These deliberate teaching practices maximize classroom and student exposure to and practice with English.

The Interaction component includes the following features:

16. Frequent opportunities for interaction and discussion between teacher and student and among students, which encourage elaborated responses about lesson concepts.

17. Grouping configurations support language and content objectives of the lesson.

18. Sufficient wait time for student responses consistently provided.

19. Ample opportunities for students to clarify key concepts in L1 as needed with aide, peer, or L1 text.

Ideas and Activities for Promoting Classroom Interaction

Is It Complete?

SIOP® SHELTERED INSTRUCTION OBSERVATION PROTOCOL

COMPONENT: Interaction

(Adapted from Angie Medina, Long Beach Unified School District)

Grade Levels: 1–4
Subject Levels: All
Grouping Configurations: Individual, partners, small groups, whole class
Materials: Questions, sentence frames, visuals, and posted vocabulary words, if necessary

Description:

The purpose of "Is it Complete?" is to encourage interaction among students while encouraging and promoting individual thought and the use of complete sentences. Students (individually, in pairs, or as a group) are asked to respond to a particular question, and they must answer in complete sentences. After the question is asked, the teacher allows some quiet thinking time. A sentence frame should be visible for ELs who need the extra support; visual aids and posted vocabulary related to the content concepts will help students think of sentences. Once students have produced a complete sentence they should put their thumbs together and hold them up to signal to the teacher that they are finished. The sentences can then be shared with partners, small groups, and eventually the entire class.

SIOP® Connection

Content Objective:

Students will be able to (SWBAT) . . .

- Demonstrate their knowledge about (a topic) through sharing complete sentences with a partner.

Language Objectives:

Students will be able to (SWBAT) . . .

- Create sentences with subject-verb agreement when discussing (a topic, such as animal habitats).

(continued)

SIOP® Connection (continued)

• Add an *s* or *es* to the end of words to make plurals, and use the word *are* as the verb to describe them:

"A _____ *is* a_____." (Ex: "A nest is a bird's home."

"_____*s are* _____." (Ex: "Nests are found in trees.")

"A _____ *is* important because _____." (Ex: "A nest is important because birds can lay eggs in them.")

"The _____*s* are important because _____." (Ex: "The eggs are important because baby birds grow in them.")

Dinner Party

SIOP® SHELTERED INSTRUCTION OBSERVATION PROTOCOL | **COMPONENT:** Interaction

(Vogt, 2000)

Grade Levels: All (for K–2, use as a birthday or tea party)
Subject Areas: Language arts, social studies, science, math
Grouping Configuration: Small Groups
Approximate Time Involved: 1–2 periods for planning and student practice
Materials: Library and/or Internet resources for research

Description:

The idea for this activity came from a final exam that one of the authors (MaryEllen) had when she was a senior in high school way (back in the early '60's)! The course, English Literature, was taught by an extraordinary teacher, Mary McNally, and for the semester exam she asked that we respond to the following prompt:

> "Suppose you could have a dinner party for eight British authors or poets that we have studied. Who would you invite? Why would you select them? What would be the seating order of the guests at your table and why would you place them in that order? What do you think the guests would talk about during dinner? Include specific references to the authors' lives and works in your response."

The purpose of Dinner Party is for students to assume the persona of characters in novels or short stories, authors or poets, historical figures, scientists, artist, politicians, or military leaders. Alexander the Great might be engaged in conversation with Abby Hoffman, while General George Patton argues the finer points of military strategy with Jane Fonda. Although scripts can be written, improvisation is more interesting and fun. During each Dinner Party, students must include specific content for the characters and respond in character to each other as realistically and accurately as possible. It is important that knowledge of people's lives, accomplishments, flaws, and works be used to inform the performance.

Young students may have a birthday or tea party and include their favorite characters from stories or nursery rhymes. If you model how a character might act at a party prior to students choosing "guests," ELs are more likely to understand the purpose of the activity.

SIOP® Connection

Content Objective:

Students will be able to (SWBAT) . . .

- Assume the persona of a character (fictional or real) and represent his or her unique history, personality, and characteristics.

Language Objective:

Students will be able to (SWBAT) . . .

- Talk about (perhaps with a partner) their characters' accomplishments and other personal facts during a pretend dinner, birthday or tea party.

Group Response with a White Board

COMPONENT: Interaction

Grade Levels: All (for K, use pictures, illustrations, numbers, or words in a multiple choice format)
Subject Levels: All
Grouping Configurations: Individual, small groups, whole class
Materials: Individual white boards; white board marking pens; paper and pencils

Description:

Group Response with a White Board fosters interaction while promoting individual thought. Students are grouped heterogeneously and each group is given a number. Each student in the group has paper and pencil, and each team has a white board and marking pen. The teacher then asks a question about a topic the class has been studying.

After allowing sufficient wait-time, ask students to individually jot down their responses to a question, even if it's a "best guess" answer. Cue team members to share their responses with each other, and students then determine the best response and a student recorder writes it on the white board. It is important that all team members help each other by making sure each student knows the answer. When all teams have written on their white boards, the teacher spins a spinner or rolls a die and according to the number, one group holds up their white board to share their answer with the rest of the class. Each team must support its answer. If the answer is wrong, emphasize that it was a *team* response that was incorrect. Spin or roll the die to select another team until the correct answer appears on a white board. The team (and class) then discuss the question and answer so that everyone is able to answer it correctly. Team points can be awarded. Group Response with a White Board is a wonderful way for students to assess their own understanding of key concepts in a low-risk environment.

SIOP® Connection

Content Objectives:

Students will be able to (SWBAT) . . .

- Demonstrate knowledge about (a topic).
- Work with teammates to devise the best possible answer to a question about (a topic).
- Evaluate team members' individual responses for accuracy.

(continued)

SIOP® Connection *(continued)*

Language Objective:

Students will be able to (SWBAT) . . .

- Orally defend their team's choice for a particular response, by using the following sentence stems:

    "We agree that _____ is the best answer because _____."

    "We came to consensus that _____ is the best answer because _____."

Reader-Writer-Speaker Response Triads

SIOP® | **COMPONENT:** Interaction

Grade Levels: All (K–1 use illustrations for jobs)
Subject Levels: All
Grouping Configurations: Partners, small groups, whole class
Materials: Construction paper; marking pen; pencil or pen

Description:

The purpose of Reader-Writer-Speaker Response Triads is to give students the opportunity to read, write, listen, and speak to each other while working in a small group. The key to this activity is that each triad can only use one paper and one writing utensil (pencil/pen/marker). Assign each student to a triad; each student takes a turn reading, writing (recording), and speaking (reporting the answer). Everyone in the triad helps the other team members: the reader reads an article, chapter, or adapted text; the writer (recorder) writes or draws the group's response; the speaker (reporter) shares the group's responses with the other class members. This activity can be used for brainstorming (e.g., naming all the proper nouns they know), for review (e.g., writing all the fact families they know), or even for drawing the cycle of something (e.g., the water cycle). This can also be used for test preparation.

Barbara Formoso (Gunston Middle School, Arlington, VA) makes simple construction paper "tents" in three different colors. Each group has one Reader tent, one Writer tent, and one Speaker tent; the tents are then rotated among each student within the triad based on the lesson's objectives.

> ## 🧭 SIOP® Connection
>
> ### Content Objectives:
>
> Students will be able to (SWBAT) . . .
>
> - Summarize three key reasons why the Confederacy chose to secede from the Union.
> - Work effectively in a group, sharing their knowledge and understandings about the causes of the Civil War.
>
> ### Language Objective:
>
> Students will be able to (SWBAT) . . .
>
> - Read an article, write a response to it, listen to triad members' ideas, and discuss why the Confederacy chose to secede from the Union.

Inside-Outside Circle*

SIOP® SHELTERED INSTRUCTION OBSERVATION PROTOCOL

COMPONENT: Interaction

(Kagan, 1994)

(*or Conga Line, with two lines of students facing each other)

Grade Levels: All
Subject Levels: All
Grouping Configurations: partners, small groups, whole class
Materials: Information for students to share orally (written information, pictures, illustrations, white boards, etc.)

Description:

The purpose of Inside-Outside Circle is to promote practice with key content concepts and develop oral language. The class is divided into two groups; half the class forms a circle looking out (the inside circle), and the other half stands in front of someone in the inner circle (the outside circle). (Younger students often do better in this activity if they are seated in the two circles.) The students are asked a question or directed to perform a task. The students in the inner circle answer first while the outer circle listens; then the outer circle responds while the inner circle listens. When each has finished, students can give a signal (e.g., thumbs up) to indicate they are finished. Once both have shared, the teacher gives a signal (e.g., ringing a bell) and the inner circle stays in place while the outer circle rotates one person clockwise.

As students rotate through the Inside-Outside Circle, the inside circle students share a piece of writing while the outside circle students act as editors. With each rotation, the editors have an assigned task, perhaps to check punctuation. The outside circle continues to rotate while helping to revise the stories that are being read by the inside circle. The roles then change and the inside circle members become the editors while the outside circle members share their writing.

SIOP® Connection

Content Objective:

Students will be able to (SWBAT) . . .

- Edit and revise their writing with the help of a partner.

SIOP® Connection *(continued)*

Language Objective:

Students will be able to (SWBAT) . . .

- Help revise another student's writing by using *praise* and *suggestion* sentence frames such as:

    "I like how you _____."

    "Did you think about _____?"

    "The best part is how you _____."

Find Your Match

SIOP® COMPONENT: Interaction

SHELTERED INSTRUCTION OBSERVATION PROTOCOL

Grade Levels: All
Subject Levels: All
Grouping Configurations: Partners, small groups, whole class
Materials: An index card for each student

Description:

Find Your Match encourages interaction among class members as they read and produce oral language. Each student is given an index card with information on it that matches the information on another students' card (e.g., words and definitions; antonyms or synonyms; generals and battles; characters and story titles, math problems and solutions, etc).

In the first step, students mix with each other, reading aloud the information on their cards. After students have had several opportunities to share their information, the teacher calls time. At that point, students are to find their matches by *describing* (not reading) what is on their cards. If students are learning about geometric shapes, student #1 has the word *parallelogram* written on his card, and student #2 has the *definition* of parallelogram on hers. While searching for their matches, student #1 listens to student #2 use her own words to describe a parallelogram. When the two students with a match find each other, they move to the side of the room until everyone is finished. At that point, all partners read both of their cards to the rest of the class.

SIOP® Connection

Content Objective:

Students will be able to (SWBAT) . . .

- Match words and/or concepts about (a topic, such as the geometric shapes).

Language Objectives:

Students will be able to (SWBAT) . . .

- Orally read the word(s) on their cards to other students.
- Describe a concept that is written on a card to another student.

Jigsaw What You Know

SIOP® | **COMPONENT:** Interaction

Grade Levels: All
Subject Levels: All
Grouping Configurations: Small groups, whole class
Materials: Index cards, labels with words or pictures

Description:

Jigsaw What You Know encourages interaction among class members through learning about a topic, classifying it within a whole, and teaching others about a dimension of the whole. Choose a topic that has 2–4 possible dimensions or qualities (e.g., animals, food); assign each dimension to a specific area in the classroom and label each area with pictures or words representing the dimension. (Assign students an area through index cards that have words or pictures related to one of the particular dimensions/qualities.) Place resources related to the topic in each designated area. Tell students to use the resources to learn about the particular dimension and decide how to best represent that dimension for their peers.

If for example, the topic of study is the Food Pyramid, divide the class into six groups (protein, fats, dairy, fruits, vegetables, grains). Each student's index card has a picture or label for a different food. Students go to the food group that is appropriate for the food on their card. After they have read together an article about their food group (e.g., protein), students use the information to create a small poster that explains the food group (e.g., what proteins are, how they contribute to good health, examples of various types of protein, etc.). Each group will then teach the rest of the class about their food group and add their poster to the whole-class chart on the Food Pyramid.

> ## 🔍 SIOP® Connection
>
> **Content Objectives:**
>
> Students will be able to (SWBAT) . . .
>
> - Classify foods into one of six food groups.
> - Create a poster that will be used to teach the other five teams about their food group.
>
> *(continued)*

SIOP® Connection *(continued)*

Language Objective:

Students will be able to (SWBAT) . . .

- Describe a food to their team using an adjective and noun:

    "The _____ (adjective) _____ (noun) belongs to the _____ group."

    ("The yellow banana belongs to the fruit group.")

    ("The creamy yogurt belongs to the dairy group.")

Gallery Walk

SIOP® SHELTERED INSTRUCTION OBSERVATION PROTOCOL

COMPONENT: Interaction

Grade Levels: 2–12
Subject Levels: All
Grouping Configurations: Individual, partners, small groups, whole class
Materials: Chart paper and marking pens

Description:

Gallery Walk promotes reflection, interaction among class members, and written and oral language development. Assign students to groups of four or five. Multiple charts are posted around the room with a particular question or topic written across the top. Each group of students begins one of the charts, focusing on its particular topic or question. Using a marking pen of a different color from the other groups, each group lists two or three ideas or responses on the chart. Groups are given three or four minutes at each chart paper, and then they rotate to the next chart, reading the other groups' contributions and adding additional information with their own colored marking pen. Groups may question or react to information written by previous groups. Groups then return to their original chart, read what the others have written, and summarize orally all of the responses for the class members; questions may be answered, points clarified, and the teacher may lead a whole class discussion on the topic.

SIOP® Connection

Content Objective:

Students will be able to (SWBAT) . . .

- Work together to respond in writing to questions and comments about (a topic) that are written on chart paper.

Language Objectives:

Students will be able to (SWBAT) . . .

- Ask questions in writing about (a topic) in response to what other students have written on the chart paper.
- Orally summarize information about (a topic) that was written on their chart paper.

Take a Stand

SIOP® | COMPONENT: Interaction

Grade Levels: All

Subject Levels: Social studies (including current events), language arts, literature, health

Grouping Configurations: Individual, partners, small groups, whole class

Materials: None

Description:

Take a Stand enables the teacher to quickly assess students' comprehension of a lesson and the ELs to practice their listening skills. Begin by making a statement to the students related to a current event, a story or novel, an issue related to students' health, etc. Permit quiet time for thinking and then give the cue, "Take a Stand," asking students to stand if they agree with the statement and stay seated if they disagree. Students must be prepared to explain their rationale for agreeing or disagreeing with the statement.

Take a Stand can also be a team activity with five or six teams. The team first discusses the statement made by the teacher, comes to consensus on whether they will sit or stand, and on cue, the entire team stands or stays seated. They then explain their rationale for agreeing or disagreeing. An adaptation to this activity is to allow students themselves to create the statements used for agreeing or disagreeing and ask the rest of the class to respond.

SIOP® Connection

Content Objective:

Students will be able to (SWBAT) . . .

- Agree or disagree with positions about (a topic, e.g., with positions of politicians related to a current event) and provide a rationale for their decision.

Language Objective:

Students will be able to (SWBAT) . . .

- Respectfully agree or disagree with other class members' perspectives about (a topic), using the sentence frames:

    "I respectfully disagree with _____ because
    _____."

    "I agree with _____ because _____."

Frozen Moment

SIOP® COMPONENT: Interaction (and Practice/Application)

(Schultz, 1998; Vogt, 2000)

Grade Levels: All
Subject Levels: Language arts, social studies, science
Grouping Configurations: Individual, partners, small groups, whole class
Materials: A piece of literature; strips of paper with sentences from story

Description:

Begin by reading a piece of literature connected to content, such as Allen Say's *Grandfather's Journey* (1993), a beautiful book about a Chinese immigrant family. After reading the story, distribute to each group of four or five students a piece of paper that has a three-or four-sentence scene taken from the story. Give each group a few minutes to plan a re-creation of the scene in pantomime, requiring, that the scene be delivered with absolutely no movement (similar to a tableau), and each person in the group must assume a role. The roles may be characters (such as the grandfather or grandmother) or stage props (such as the cherry tree, ship, or waves). After sufficient time to practice, students create their "frozen moments" while the rest of the class members close their eyes. When ready, class members open their eyes to view the scene and attempt to identify the particular scene being portrayed.

After the students have viewed the scene for a few minutes, the teacher joins the performers, tapping one of the actors, who then "comes to life." In character, this student describes what he or she is thinking or feeling at that moment. For example, the ship crossing the ocean might say, "I am so tired. I've now been to sea for weeks and I've been tossed about by huge waves and fierce storms. I must stay afloat to save my passengers." The teacher ends the soliloquy by again tapping the student, who returns to the fixed, still position. Others players in the scene may be tapped until class members have correctly identified the scene that is being performed.

Even if the rest of the students think they can identify the scene, it's important to let several cast members come to life during the re-creation. Much of the fun in this activity is watching the "frozen moment" come to life; this part of the process should not be rushed.

🔍 SIOP® Connection

Content Objectives:

Students will be able to (SWBAT) . . .

- Read about a scene in a story, and with peers re-enact the scene as a tableau, including key characters, events, and settings.
- Watch a tableau to determine which scene the actors are portraying.

(continued)

SIOP® Connection (continued)

Language Objectives:

Students will be able to (SWBAT) . . .

- Orally describe the roles they are playing in the tableau by assuming a character or element of the setting.
- Listen to characters in the tableau in order to determine the scene they are portraying.
- "Come to life" as a character or other figure, improvising what the character or figure might say at that moment in time.

You Are There

SHELTERED INSTRUCTION
SIOP®
OBSERVATION PROTOCOL

COMPONENT: Interaction (and Practice/Application)

(Vogt, 2000)

Grade Levels: 4–12
Subject Levels: Social Studies, Math, Language Arts, Science
Grouping Configurations: Small groups, whole class
Materials: Resources (books, articles, websites) for research

Description:

This activity is based upon the classic television program *You Are There*, hosted by Edward R. Murrow, in which characters involved in actual historical events were interviewed about their involvement and participation in the event. The re-creations were historically accurate, and the historical figures came alive for viewers

In preparation for You Are There in the classroom, groups of students conduct research on the event they will be portraying. Having completed their research, the students select a character that played a crucial role in the event and write interview questions and responses that an interviewer will use during the dramatic re-enactment. Students could interview Sacajawea, the Shoshone guide and interpreter who accompanied Lewis and Clark on their expedition, or interview the Wright brothers upon their arrival at Kitty Hawk, North Carolina. Both the interviewer and the interviewee are apprised of all questions and responses prior to the performance.

Another dimension can be added to this activity, especially if you are working with older high school students: audience members direct unrehearsed questions to the central character. Obviously, all students, including the interviewee, must have a thorough knowledge of the event for this to be a successful activity.

SIOP® Connection

Content Objectives:

Students will be able to (SWBAT) . . .

- Demonstrate their understanding of a person or historical event by creating interview questions and responses.
- Convey the essence of the person or historical event through an interview that is performed for peers.

Language Objectives:

Students will be able to (SWBAT) . . .

- Write interview questions.
- Create appropriate responses to the interview questions.

Great Performances

SIOP® COMPONENT: Interaction (and Practice/Application)

SHELTERED INSTRUCTION
OBSERVATION PROTOCOL

(Vogt, 2000)

Grade Levels: 3–12
Subject Levels: Social Studies, Math, Language Arts, Science
Grouping Configurations: Small groups, whole class
Materials: Resources (books, articles, websites) for research

Description:

In this activity students act out significant events in pantomime or improvisation. Possibilities include Alexander Graham Bell's first use of a telephone, Henry Ford's realization that automation could increase the production of Model T's, or Neil Armstrong's first steps on the moon. Depending on the content and grade level, students select an event that is very well known or one that is interesting and important but not as famous. In pairs students conduct research on their selected topic, learning as much as possible about the specific sequence of events leading up to the Great Performance.

With an activity such as this, it may be easier to start students with pantomime, move to improvisation with speaking, and then on to writing and performing brief scripts. Students (including English learners who are shy about speaking in front of peers) can effectively and creatively pantomime events and situations. Through pantomime students learn how to communicate with facial expressions, body language and position, and movement.

> ## SIOP® Connection
>
> **Content Objective:**
>
> Students will be able to (SWBAT) . . .
>
> - Act out a sequence of events that lead to (a great moment in history).
>
> **Language Objectives:**
>
> Students will be able to (SWBAT) . . .
>
> - Plan the Great Performance using sequence words such as *first, then, next,* and *finally.*
> - Improvise a scene and speak as a character in an historical event.

Role Playing

SIOP® | **COMPONENT:** Interaction

Grade Levels: All
Subject Levels: Social Studies, Math, Language Arts, Science
Grouping Configurations: Small groups, whole class
Materials: None

Description:

When Role Playing, the teacher is directly involved in the scenarios to be created, modeling, prompting, and extending the conversation in order to provide English language practice. Students of mixed abilities and language proficiencies participate together; some may need more scaffolding than others. The role-playing activities promote language development while also developing confidence in using the new language.

Settings for Role Playing can be almost anything, depending on the age and language proficiency of the students participating: a supermarket (making correct change or selecting good produce); football game (cheering on the home team); Department of Motor Vehicles office (applying for a driver's license); the school cafeteria (ordering food); and so forth. With practice students will be able to internalize language structures that are modeled through interaction with the teacher and other students.

SIOP® Connection

Content Objective:

Students will be able to (SWBAT) . . .

- Participate in a role play scenario about (a topic).

Language Objective:

Students will be able to (SWBAT) . . .

- Create a scenario about (a topic) by engaging in conversation with the teacher and other students.

Puppetry

SIOP® — SHELTERED INSTRUCTION OBSERVATION PROTOCOL

COMPONENT: Interaction

(Vogt, 2000)

Grade Levels: K–8
Subject Levels: Social Studies, Math, Language Arts, Science
Grouping Configurations: Small groups, whole class
Materials: Hand puppets (hand-made or commercially created)

Description:

Puppetry is wonderful for beginning English speakers because it engages them in low-risk drama play. The teacher, or another student, reads aloud a story, poem, or article while students perform the actions with puppets. ELs should be encouraged to use English as much as possible because they may understand more (receptive language) than they can speak (expressive language). The puppets can demonstrate content knowledge when the student may be unable to do so verbally. Although puppets can be quite elaborate, they can also be made out of simple household materials (e.g., socks or paper lunch bags), and all students can be involved in making the puppets, stages, and scenery.

After listening to a simple story about a child going to the grocery store with his mother, a student may be able to convey his understanding of the story by pretending with his puppet to buy an artificial tomato and pay for it (with play money). By encouraging him to use simple sentences such as, "I would like a tomato, please," and, "Thank you very much," the EL is practicing English in a non-threatening way.

🔍 SIOP® Connection

Content Objective:

Students will be able to (SWBAT) . . .

- Respond to a story by using a puppet to convey their understanding.

Language Objectives:

Students will be able to (SWBAT) . . .

- Use simple English sentences and phrases as the voice of a puppet.
- Engage in a simple conversation, puppet to puppet.

The SIOP® Model: Interaction

Lesson Plans

The following lesson plans involve the activity, Find Your Match (p. 112). While the lessons incorporate all of the eight SIOP® components, the emphasis here is on Interaction. From the beginning to the end of the lesson, students are given multiple opportunities to interact with the teacher as well as with their peers. The teacher models and provides guided practice, using examples and manipulatives to allow for meaningful interaction between teacher and student. Students demonstrate understanding of the concept with their peers in pairs and small groups. Key vocabulary is used to discuss the concepts ensuring elaborated responses.

These lesson plans serve as an example; depending on your grade level and state standards, appropriate text selections and content standards can be substituted. This example is intended to demonstrate how to incorporate the Interaction component of the SIOP® Model into a lesson plan.

FIGURE 6.1 *Elementary Lesson Plan Promoting Classroom Interaction*

Key: SW = Students will; TW = Teacher will; SWBAT = Students will be able to . . . ; HOTS = Higher Order Thinking Skills

SIOP®Lesson: Geometric shapes	*Grade: 4*

Content Standard: Concept 1: Geometric Properties
Analyze the attributes and properties of 2- and 3-dimensional shapes
and develop mathematical arguments about their relationships.
Identify congruent geometric shapes.

Key Vocabulary: congruent, parallel, perpendicular, angle, polygon & quadrilateral **HOTS:** Why is it important to learn about the various shapes found in our world?	**Visuals/Resources/Supplementary Materials:** geometric shapes: overhead tiles, overhead and graph paper & index cards; Poem "Shapes" by Shel Silverstein; geoboards

Connections to Prior Knowledge/ Building Background: (10 minutes)
TW read the poem.
SW arrange geometric shapes according to what they hear in the poem.
SW then choose one shape and turn to a partner and share the number of sides and how many are the same. They will also share how the shapes are the same and how they are different.

Content Objectives:	**Meaningful Activities:**	**Review/Assessment:**
1. SWBAT demonstrate comprehension of congruent geometric shapes by replicating and labeling congruent shapes using geoboards.	**1.1** TW model on the overhead using a geoboard what one of the shapes from the poem should look like. TW describe the shape using key vocabulary.	
	1.2 SW, in pairs using their own geoboards, replicate one of the shapes they constructed earlier in the BB activity. Students will also label the angles, sides, and type of shape (polygon, quadrilateral) on an illustration of the shape.	**1.2** SW label the illustration using the words parallel, congruent, polygon etc. (key vocabulary).
	1.3 TW then add another shape to the goeboard explaining congruent shapes.	
	1.4 SW, in pairs, work with a second team using their geoboards to model congruent shapes.	**1.4** SW identify at least one congruent shape.

(continued)

FIGURE 6.1 *Elementary Lesson Plan Promoting Classroom Interaction* *(continued)*

Language Objectives:		
2. SWBAT demonstrate application of congruent geometric shapes by identifying and orally explaining characteristics (sides, angels, etc.) of triangles, rectangles squares and circles.	**2.1** TW give each student an index card. Some students will have the illustration of a geometric shape, while others will have an index card with the description of the shape (name, angles, sides). **2.2** SW, in a "Find Your Match" activity, match congruent shapes with the appropriate description.	**2.1** Students identify the appropriate match and use key vocabulary to share their match and why it is congruent with the whole group.

Wrap-up: In math journals, students will complete one cloze sentence to describe one geometric shape. For example:

1. A rectangle has _____ pairs of parallel sides, _____ pairs of equal sides, and _____right angles.

2. A triangle has _____ pairs of parallel sides, _____ equal sides, and _____pairs of congruent angles.

3. A square has _____ pairs of parallel sides, _____ equal sides, and pairs of congruent angles.

SW share their shapes and sentences with a partner.

Source: Lesson plan created by Melissa Castillo and Nicole Teyechea. Lesson content by Melissa Castillo and Kendra Moreno.

FIGURE 6.2 *Secondary Lesson Plan Promoting Classroom Interaction*

Key: SW = Students will; TW = Teacher will; SWBAT = Students will be able to . . . ; HOTS = Higher Order Thinking Skills

SIOP® Lesson: Quadrilaterals	*Grade: 9*

Content Standard: Concept 1: Geometric Properties Analyze the attributes and properties of 2- and 3- dimensional shapes and develop mathematical arguments about their relationships.
PO 2: Identify the hierarchy of quadrilaterals.

Key Vocabulary: Polygon, hierarchy, quadrilateral, parallel, parallelogram, rhombus, rectangle, square, congruent, right angle and trapezoid **HOTS:** What is similar about a 3-sided figure (triangle) and a four-sided figure (quadrilateral)? What is different about a 3-sided figure (triangle) and a 4-sided figure (quadrilateral)?	**Visuals/ Resources/Supplementary Materials:** Triangles, examples of three-sided objects and four-sided figures, overhead tiles

Connections to Prior Knowledge/Building Background Information: (10 minutes)
SW organize tiles, objects, and figures using different characteristics such as shape and number of sides; they will then do a quick-write answering the following questions:

1. What family of shapes does a triangle come from? (polygon) (Students have studied triangles in a previous lesson.)

2. What are some types of triangles? (right, acute, obtuse)

SW in a conga line (see p. 110) share their quick-writes.

FIGURE 6.2 *Secondary Lesson Plan Promoting Classroom Interaction*   (*continued*)

Content Objectives:	Meaningful Activities:	Review/Assessment:
1. SWBAT demonstrate knowledge of the hierarchy of quadrilaterals (four-sided figures) by matching a four-sided figure/shape to its appropriate name and definition.	1.1 TW use PowerPoint to illustrate different quadrilaterals. 1.2 SW, using graph paper, outline examples of quadrilaterals identifying the number of sides and angles, following the examples presented on the screen. 1.3 SW each be given an index card, some with a shape, others with the definition of the shape, the # of sides and angles. 1.4 SW in a "Find Your Match" activity match the shapes with the appropriate definition.	 1.4 SW find their match— type of quadrilateral & definition.
Language Objectives: 2. SWBAT demonstrate comprehension of the hierarchy of quadrilaterals (four-sided figures) by explaining how their four-sided figure/shape is a type of quadrilateral.	2.1 SW with their match/partner share their shape/figure and the definition explaining what makes it a quadrilateral.	2.1 SW use the words *quadrilateral, trapezoid, rectangle, square, rhombus*, etc., type of angles and sides to share with the group.

Wrap-up: In small groups SW complete one cloze sentence to describe one quadrilateral and use overhead tiles to create the quadrilateral on an overhead.

For example:

1. A rectangle has _____ pairs of parallel sides, _____ pairs of equal sides, and _____right angles.

2. A rhombus has _____ pairs of parallel sides, _____ equal sides, and _____pairs of congruent angles.

3. An isosceles trapezoid has _____ pairs of parallel sides, _____ equal sides, and pairs of congruent angles.

SW share their shape and sentences with the whole group.

Source: Lesson plan created by Melissa Castillo and Nicole Teyechea. Lesson content by Melissa Castillo and Kendra Moreno.

Practice and Application

Overview of the Practice and Application Component

It is essential that students acquiring English have multiple, daily opportunities to practice and apply what they are learning. The reasons are two-fold: 1) students are more likely to retain new information if they immediately put it to use; and 2) the teacher can assess students' learning while they are practicing and applying their new understandings. Opportunities for practicing and applying new learning must occur regularly within each lesson, not just at its conclusion. English learners especially need additional time to process because they may also be translating from their native language (L1) to English (L2). While practicing and applying, they have additional time to think about their new learning; if they are reading, writing, listening, and speaking, they will also be receiving additional and necessary practice using English.

It is desirable to provide students with hands-on practice and application. This may be in contrast to widely used worksheets and study guides that generally require a high level of English proficiency, but little language support. Manipulatives, puppets, maps, white boards, role-playing, experiments, games, projects, and so forth all allow ELs opportunities to actively practice and apply what they are learning.

The Practice and Application component includes the following features:

20. Hands-on materials and/or manipulatives provided for students to practice using new content knowledge.

21. Activities provided for students to apply content and language knowledge in the classroom.

22. Activities integrate all language skills (i.e., reading, writing, listening, and speaking).

Ideas and Activities for Providing Students with Practice and Application

In the Loop

SIOP® **COMPONENT:** Practice and Application

(Adapted from Peggy Senneff, Long Beach Unified School District)

Grade Levels: All

Subject Areas: Math, Science

Grouping Configuration: Individual, Pairs

Approximate Time Involved: About 10 minutes, depending on amount of time teacher allows and how many examples students are required to give.

Materials: Cereal in the shape of "O's"

Description:

The purpose of In the Loop is to provide hands-on practice of key concepts with manipulatives (which can later be eaten). Provide each pair of students with a piece of paper and a small paper cup of generic loops or round oats cereal. Give students a problem, anything from simple addition to cell construction, which they must demonstrate with the loops. Students should be allowed time to look at other responses and to explain their own processes before the cereal is eaten or another problem given. For example, partners decide how to place the loops to mimic the construction of a cell and then describe the process of cell division in writing.

   Note: Purchase large, discounted boxes of generic loops, and have a supply of baby wipes or anti-bacterial hand lotion available for students to use before the activity.

SIOP® Connection

Content Objective:

Students will be able to (SWBAT) . . .

- Demonstrate understanding of (a topic, e.g., the construction of a cell) through the use of loops.

Language Objective:

Students will be able to (SWBAT) . . .

- Use prepositions and prepositional phrases when describing to their partners how and where to place the Loops: *next to, on top of, between, under, near, behind,* and *below.*

Bingo

SIOP® COMPONENT: Practice and Application

Grade Levels: All

Subject Areas: All

Grouping Configuration: Individual

Approximate Time Involved: About 15 minutes

Materials: Piece of paper for each student; paper squares or cereal shaped in O's

Description:

The purpose of Bingo is to provide students with hands-on practice with words or facts. Model for students how to fold a blank piece of newsprint into 9(3 × 3) or 16(4 × 4) squares and display 10–20 vocabulary words (or math facts). Students fill in the squares in random order so that no two are identical. The teacher passes out paper squares (which can be collected and saved for the next Bingo game) or loop cereal (which can be eaten after the lesson). While the game is in session, do not call out the exact word or fact the students have written, but a definition or related fact instead. Students have to find the match and cover the square on the Bingo sheet with the small paper square or cereal O.

If students have written *cell,* the teacher says, "This is a very small unit of living matter." If the students have written the number *7,* the teacher says, "This is the square root of 49." Students can also say the definition aloud so that other class members have to determine the word being defined. This activity may be carried out over the course of two days: On the first day, students answer each clue and write it in a random square; on the second day, students play the game.

SIOP® Connection

Content Objective:

Students will be able to (SWBAT) . . .

- Identify, define, and use vocabulary related to (a topic).

Language Objectives:

Students will be able to (SWBAT) . . .

- Use listening, speaking, reading, and writing to learn key vocabulary related to (a topic).
- Determine if (a vocabulary word) is a common noun or a proper noun and use either lower case or upper case letters to write it (e.g., for a lesson on the Solar System, vocabulary could include *rocks, sun, moon, planets, orbit, satellite, Pluto, Venus, Earth, Mars,* and *Saturn*).

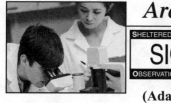

Are You Sleeping?

COMPONENT: Practice and Application

(Adapted from Peggy Senneff, Long Beach Unified School District)

Grade Levels: K–5

Subject Areas: All

Grouping Configuration: Partners, small groups, whole class

Approximate Time Involved: 15–20 minutes depending on how much of the language is scaffolded by the teacher

Materials: Chart paper

Description:

With Are You Sleeping?, students practice what they are learning by singing familiar melodies. For example, many students know the melody to the song, "Are You Sleeping?" Guide students in summarizing key content information into four or eight phrases that fit the melody; the lyrics can be written on charts so that on subsequent days the whole class can sing them together. Students can use a variety of resources (texts, poems, vocabulary lists, picture books, websites) to assist them in creating the songs.

In a unit on weather, for example, the teacher can brainstorm, post, and discuss weather-related terms such as *stormy, blowing, cloudy, rain, cold, hot,* and so forth. Using the tune, "Are You Sleeping?" students might create a song like the following:

"Is it stormy?

Is it stormy?

Yes, it is!

Yes, it is!

See the wind is blowing,

See the leaves are falling,

See the clouds,

Hear the rain."

More vocabulary related to the weather can be substituted to create additional verses. Some English learners, depending on their native country, may not be familiar with nursery rhymes and folk songs that are indigenous to the United States: Remember to teach the original song (e.g, "Are You Sleeping?") prior to replacing the lyrics with those generated by the class.

> ## SIOP® Connection
>
> **Content Objective:**
> Students will be able to (SWBAT) . . .
>
> - Create songs based on the key concepts related to (a topic).
>
> *(continued)*

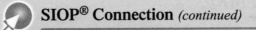

SIOP® Connection *(continued)*

Language Objective:

Students will be able to (SWBAT) . . .

- Generate vocabulary related to (a topic) and create phrases that can be sung to a familiar melody.

Poetry and Patterns

SIOP® | **COMPONENT:** Practice and Application

(Contributed by David J. Larwa, Educational Consultant)

Grade Levels: 5–12

Subject Areas: Math, science

Grouping Configuration: Small groups

Approximate Time Involved: One class period (depending on the background of the students)

Materials: Vocabulary word lists

Description:

This activity reviews and reinforces vocabulary words in mathematics and science. Students in cooperative groups use vocabulary words to write one Haiku for each group member. The Haiku can be written as a true or false statement. The pattern for Haiku is:

- Five syllables
- Seven syllables
- Five syllables

Begin by reviewing a unit's vocabulary words. Have students write out their reasoning in true or false form, and then instruct each group to write Haikus for each vocabulary word. Groups share their poems with the class and the class determines whether they are true or false.

True Example

(Vocabulary word: *variable,* a letter that represents a number)

> *A variable*
> *Any letter (x) will do*
> *An unknown number*

(Vocabulary word: *variable expression,* an equation containing a variable)

> *The equation is*
> *Variable expression*
> *2x = 6*

False Example

(Vocabulary word: *ratio,* a comparison of two numbers or quantities)

> *Ratios compare*
> *Too, a colon, or fraction*
> *Can be simplified*

Next Steps: Tanka

Tanka is a Japanese poetic form that consists of 31 syllables (5-7-5-7-7). It is the most fundamental poetic form in Japan and Haiku is derived from it. Have students write a Tanka after studying a science topic, as in the one below from earth science.

ring of fire earthquake

they have taken many lives

tsunami water

too far away to notice

death and damage at my door

For more ideas about using poetry in the content areas, read *Practical Poetry: A Nonstandard Approach to Meeting Content-Area Standards* (2005) by Sara Holbrook, Portsmouth, NH: Heinemann.

Go Graphic for Expository Texts

COMPONENT: Practice and Application

Grade Levels: 3–10

Subject Areas: All

Grouping Configuration: Partners, small groups, whole class

Approximate Time Involved: 10–20 minutes

Materials: Graphic organizers (see Figures 7.1–7.6)

Description:

Go Graphic encourages organized thought processes through the use of graphic organizers that correspond to a variety of text structures. The first step in the process is teaching students that authors write expository text in ways that often reflect the content they are describing. Graphic organizers that mirror how the text is written can help students better understand how to read and learn the material. Model how to identify the type of text structure by showing many different examples; one by one, introduce the graphic organizers that best match the text examples.

After introducing graphic organizers to the class, ask students (in partners or groups) to select the appropriate organizer (based on the structure of a text the group reads together), and use it to organize the content. Once students have completed the organizers, ask them to write a summary paragraph (or sentences) about the text.

As an example, the most common text structures found in expository texts (nonfiction and informational) include the following:

- Explanation (main idea and supporting details)
- Cause and Effect
- Comparison and Contrast
- Sequence or chronological
- Problem/Solution
- Description

(See Figures 7.1–7.6 for examples of each organizer.)

SIOP® Connection

Content Objective (as an example for a character study):

Students will be able to (SWBAT) . . .

- Depict the life of (a character) in graphic and written form.

(continued)

> ### SIOP® Connection (continued)
>
> **Language Objective:**
>
> Students will be able to (SWBAT) . . .
>
> - Use regular and irregular past-tense verbs (e.g., *born, lived, graduated, married, had, invented, died*) to describe the different phases of (a character's) life that are represented on the timeline.

Explanation: Main Idea and Supporting Details.

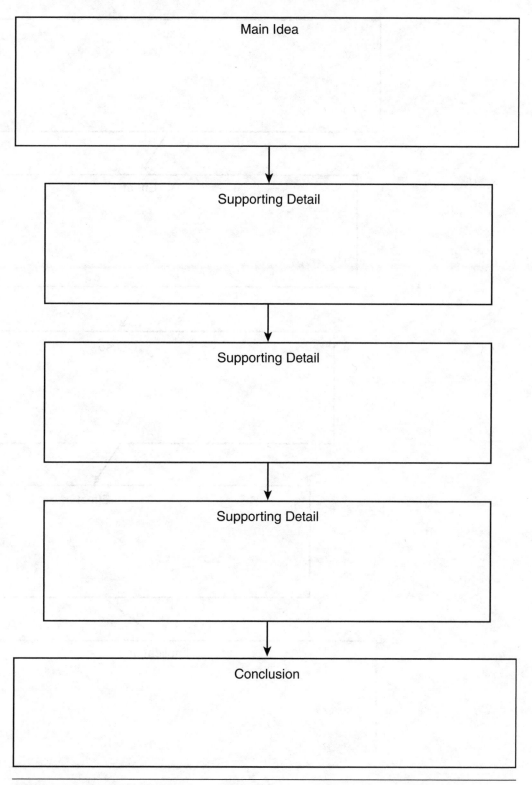

FIGURE 7.1 *Main Idea and Supporting Details*

This organizer can also be used to help students learn how to write a simple paragraph. The Main Idea becomes the topic sentence and the Conclusion becomes the concluding sentence.

Source: © 2006 Pearson Achievement Solutions, a division of Pearson Education. All rights reserved.

Cause and Effect

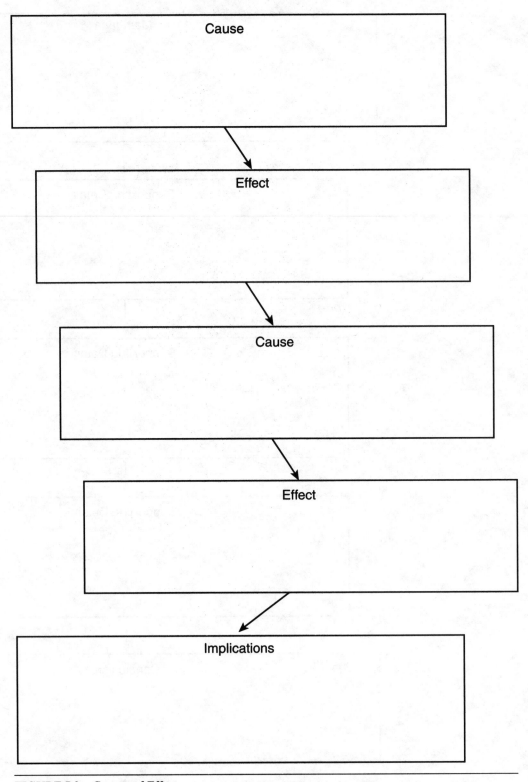

FIGURE 7.2 *Cause and Effect*

Compare and Contrast

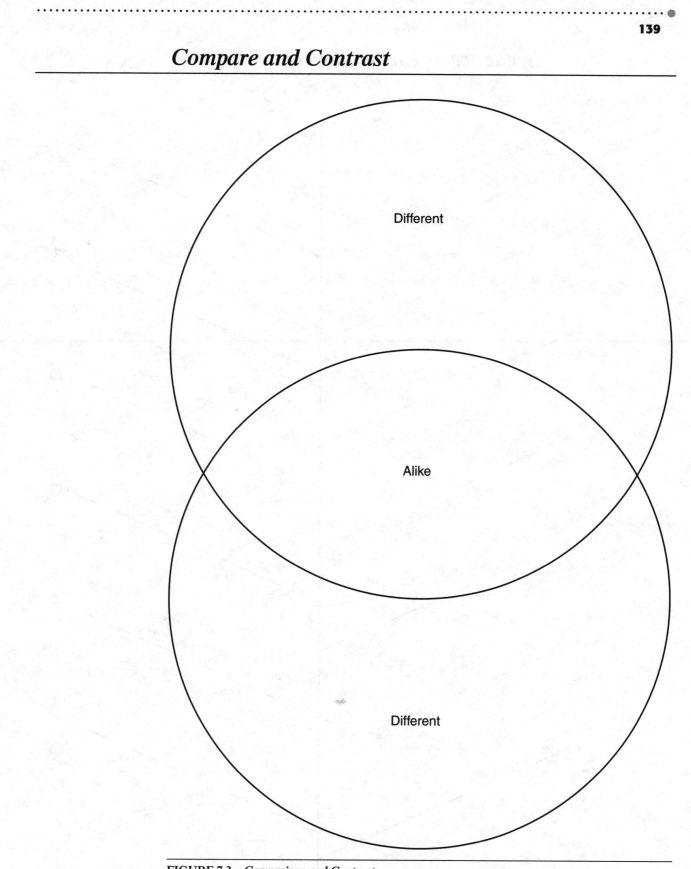

Different

Alike

Different

FIGURE 7.3 *Comparison and Contrast*

Source: © 2006 Pearson Achievement Solutions, a division of Pearson Education. All rights reserved.

Sequence or Chronological

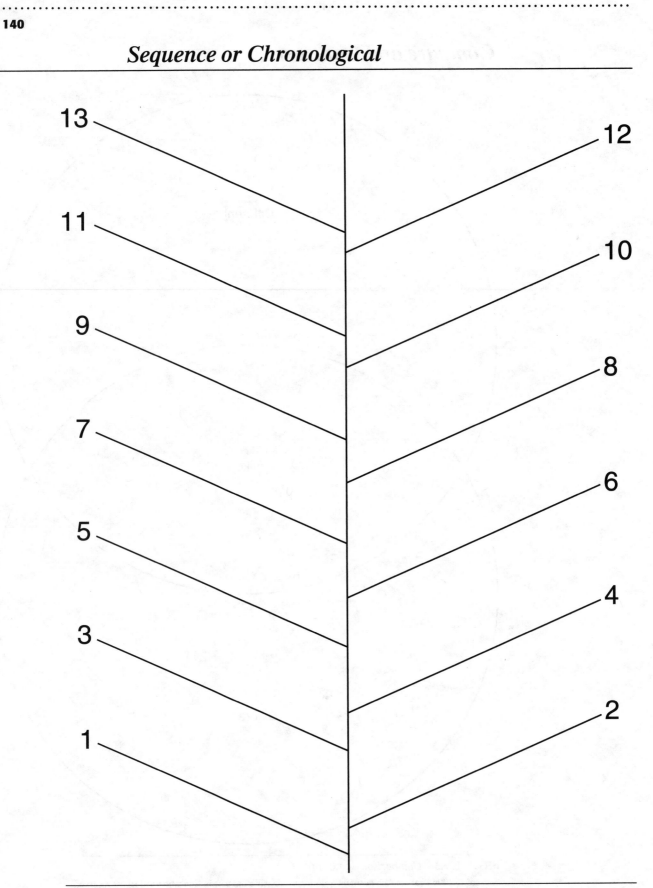

FIGURE 7.4 *Sequence or Chronological*

Source: © 2006 Pearson Achievement Solutions, a division of Pearson Education. All rights reserved.

Problem/Solution

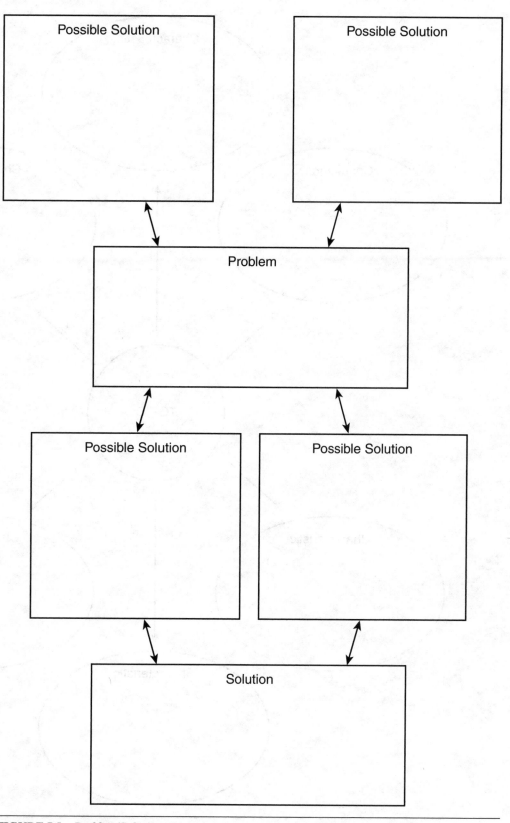

FIGURE 7.5 *Problem/Solution*

Ideas and Activities for Providing Students with Practice and Application

Description

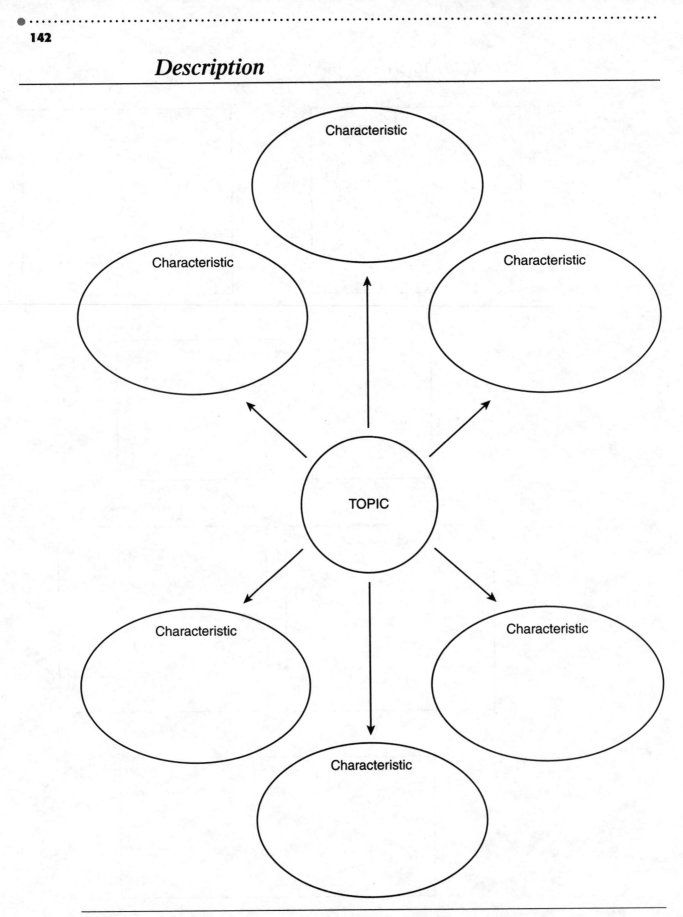

FIGURE 7.6 *Description*

Plot Chart

COMPONENT: Practice and Application

(Macon, Buell, & Vogt, 1991)

Grade Levels: K–5

Subject Areas: Language Arts and other subjects (when stories/narrative texts are read)

Grouping Configuration: Partners, small groups, whole class

Approximate Time Involved: 10–30 minutes, depending on the length of story

Materials: Chart paper for whole class Plot Chart; individual Plot Charts for seat work; short story

Description:

The Plot Chart you see in Figure 7.7 is an adaptation of an earlier version created by the late Dr. Barbara Schmidt, a wonderful teacher's teacher. In her original Plot Chart (specifically for K–2), there were just four boxes: *Somebody, Wanted, But, So.* The version you see here is a bit more sophisticated to be appropriate for complex stories; we encourage you to use either version, depending on your students' needs.

Begin by telling students a familiar fairy tale. Model how to use the Plot Chart with the whole class, and together complete the graphic organizer. Then read a story aloud (or have students read a story); and have them complete the Plot Chart. Eventually, with practice, students can use either of the Plot Charts (short or longer form) to plan their own stories. The Plot Chart is very effective as a pre-writing tool for organizing thoughts prior to writing a short story.

SIOP® Connection

Content Objective:

Students will be able to (SWBAT) . . .

- Recreate the sequence of the story, using a Plot Chart, after reading (or listening to) a short story.

Language Objective:

Students will be able to (SWBAT) . . .

- Orally summarize the plot of a short story using the completed Plot Chart.

Somebody

wanted

so

but

so

In the end,

FIGURE 7.7 *Plot Chart*

Source: Adapted from Schmidt, Macon, Buell, & Vogt, 1991. © 2006 Pearson Achievement Solutions, a division of Pearson Education. All rights reserved.

Short Story Flow Chart

SIOP® SHELTERED INSTRUCTION OBSERVATION PROTOCOL

COMPONENT: Practice and Application

(Created by MaryEllen Vogt)

> Grade Levels: Grades 3–10
>
> Subject Areas: Language Arts and other subjects (when stories/narrative texts are read)
>
> Grouping Configuration: Partners, small groups, whole class
>
> Approximate Time Involved: 10–30 minutes, depending on the length of story
>
> Materials: Copies of the Short Story Flow Chart

Description:

In the activity Go Graphic (p. 135), teachers are encouraged to show students how to organize information using specific graphic organizers for six common expository text structures. Although the Short Story Flow Chart (see Figure 7.8) has the same purpose, it is intended for narrative (fiction) texts, particularly picture books or short stories. Internalizing the elements of a short story is needed in order to develop comprehension. The main elements (characters; setting; plot: beginning, middle, ending) are included in the Short Story Flow Chart, along with the opportunity to make a prediction (What happens next?) and evaluate (What was your favorite part? What was something you learned?).

The Flow Chart also helps students learn how to summarize the essential information in a short story. After reading a story aloud, teach students how to determine the most important events that occurred in the beginning, middle, and end of the story. In the early stages of working with the Short Story Flow Chart, students will want to include all details: Stay firm; when students are required to write the essential information only in the box provided they eventually learn to be selective and purposeful about what they write.

Model use of the Short Story Flow Chart several times before having students complete it independently. Like the Plot Chart, the Short Story Flow Chart works well as a prewriting activity when students are learning to write their own short stories.

📡 SIOP® Connection

Content and Language Objectives:

Students will be able to (SWBAT) . . .

- Identify a short story's elements (title, author, setting, main characters, and sequence of events) using a Short Story Flow Chart.

- Evaluate the extent to which they enjoyed the short story, and provide a rationale for their rating on the Short Story Flow Chart.

- Write in three sentences the beginning, middle, and end of a short story they have read.

- Describe the main character of a short story with adjectives other than "nice" and "good."

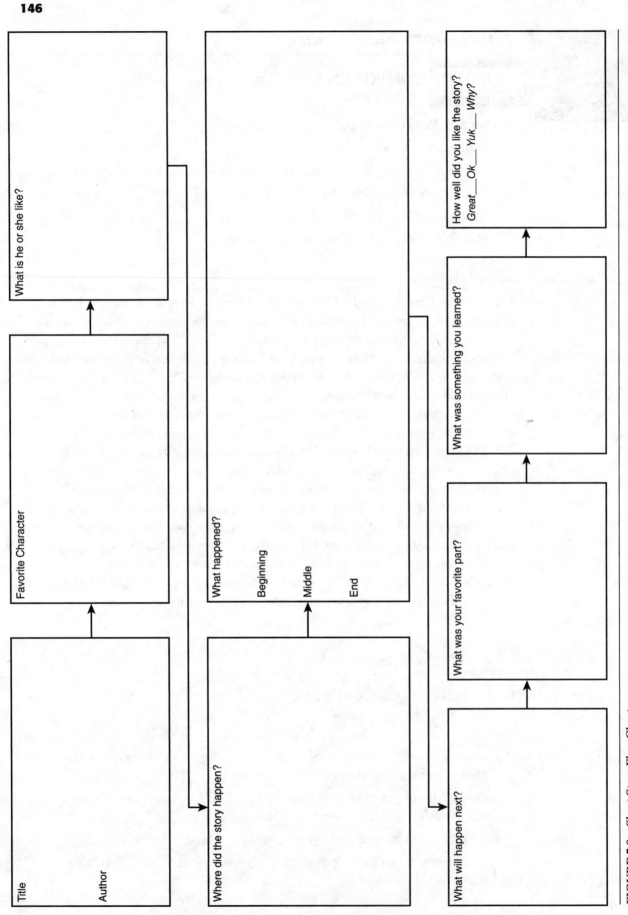

FIGURE 7.8 Short Story Flow Chart
Source: MaryEllen Vogt.

The Frame Up

COMPONENT: Practice and Application

(Adapted from Long Beach Unified School District)

Grade Levels: 2–8

Subject Areas: All

Grouping Configuration: Groups of 2 or 4

Approximate Time Involved: 15 minutes for the main activity, plus 5 to 10 minutes for sharing after the activity or on the next day

Materials: The frames (see Figure 7.9); resources for research (e.g., books, articles, websites)

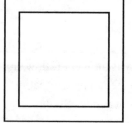

FIGURE 7.9 *The Frame Up*

Source: © 2006 Pearson Achievement Solutions, a division of Pearson Education. All rights reserved.

Description:

The purpose of The Frame Up is to help students sort the components of a concept (e.g, four habitats that make up a region, four components of a healthy diet, four types of mammals, or four types of vegetables). The teacher distributes two pieces of construction paper, one to be used as a frame, to each group (four or five students). The central topic is written in the center of one of the construction papers. Students take turns passing the frame around as each student asks (interviews) the others about their ideas for filling in one side of the frame. A second student asks the group for ideas on filling in the second side of the frame, and so on. Later the students can be assigned to write what they learned about the topic, using the frame as an organizer. The frames are presented to the other teams to share the information gathered.

For example, with the name of a region (e.g., Northwest) written in the center of the frame, students pass the frame around the group, discuss, and then write about four habitats related to each region on the four sides of the frame. Students should have access to various classroom resources to facilitate the completion of the frame. The Frame-Up works as a culminating activity when information has been gathered previously.

SIOP® Connection

Content Objective:

Students will be able to (SWBAT) . . .

- Orally and in writing share information about four components of (a topic).

Language Objectives:

Students will be able to (SWBAT) . . .

- Use comparative adjectives in the creation of their frames about (a topic) and four of its components.
- Add *–er* and *–est* to adjectives to compare and contrast (the descriptions of the four components).

Piece O' pizza

SIOP® **COMPONENT:** Practice and Application (and Strategies)

Grade Levels: 2–12

Subject Areas: All

Grouping Configuration: Partners, small groups

Approximate Time Involved: 15 minutes.

Materials: A large circle drawn on construction paper and cut into eight pieces (slices)

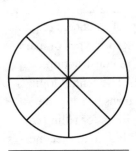

FIGURE 7.10 *Piece O' Pizza*

Source: © 2006 Pearson Achievement Solutions, a division of Pearson Education. All rights reserved.

Description:

Piece O'Pizza demonstrates how parts make up a whole. This activity is an ideal follow-up for a jigsaw reading activity during which each group of students has been given a section of an article or chapter to read. It is also helpful to use Piece O' Pizza when teaching about a concept, idea, or object that has many parts. Cut a large circle into slices with each slice given to a small group of students. Groups decorate their slice with information bits and illustrations (when appropriate). The pizza is later reassembled as the groups share their information. Students can then choose or be assigned a slice to write about or illustrate in more detail.

As an example, each group is assigned one battle of the U.S Civil War to depict and explain on a slice of the pizza. The groups include important details relevant to the respective battles, and the information is shared by the team with the whole class, then placed together with the other pieces of information to form the Civil War Pizza.

SIOP® Connection

Content Objectives:

Students will be able to (SWBAT) . . .

- Describe eight components of (the topic).
- Summarize information about (one component, e.g., one Civil War battle).

Language Objective:

Students will be able to (SWBAT) . . .

- Use past tense verbs to describe battles of the Civil War. (Note that verb tense may differ depending on the content topic; if the topic is a current event, the tense will be present. You may also focus on some other aspect of language development.)

Virginia Reel*

*Similar to a CONGA LINE

SIOP® **COMPONENT:** Practice and Application (and Interaction)

Grade Levels: All

Subject Areas: All

Grouping Configuration: Partners

Approximate Time Involved: 10–15 minutes

Materials: Index cards or paper

Description:

Virginia Reel gives ELs a chance to review or practice newly learned information. They form two lines facing each other; one line of students has a question, statement, or problem written on an index card, along with the answer (e.g., a spelling word, a math equation, a word problem, a clue to a story character, a vocabulary word and definition, a description of an historical occurrence, etc.). One student reads the word, equation, or clue to his or her partner, waits for a response, and then checks to see if the response is correct. At the teacher's cue, one line then shifts one partner to the right while the person on the end goes around to the beginning of the line to meet the person now without a partner. After the students with cards have asked several students, they hand the cards to their partners who then move again to the right and ask a new partner. This activity can be repeated a number of times so that students are exposed to as many of the cards as possible. The teacher and students then discuss areas of confusion that arose during the Virginia Reel and clarification is then made for the entire class.

For example, during a Virginia Reel, one half of the students have cards with an idiom on one side and its meaning on the other. Students holding the card read the idiomatic expression to a partner and the partner guesses the true meaning of the phrase. The first student then confirms the student's guess or gives the correct meaning. The students then exchange cards and move on to another partner.

> ### 🧭 SIOP® Connection
>
> **Content Objective** (for idiomatic expressions):
> Students will be able to (SWBAT) . . .
>
> - Identify idiomatic expressions and their meanings.
>
> **Language Objective:**
> Students will be able to (SWBAT) . . .
>
> *(continued)*

SIOP® Connection (continued)

- Use the following sentence frames when making guesses about the meaning of idiomatic expressions:

"I think _____ means _____."

"My guess is that _____ means _____."

"My idea is that _____ means _____."

"My thought is that _____ means _____."

Numbered Heads Together

COMPONENT: Practice and Application

(Kagan, 1994)

Grade Levels: 3–12

Subject Areas: All

Grouping Configuration: Small groups within a whole class setting

Approximate Time Involved: 30–45 minutes

Materials: A numbered spinner

Description:

Numbered Heads Together provides students with practice in reviewing material prior to an exam (or other assessment), and encourages the sharing of information so that all students can master the content and language objectives related to a content topic. Students are grouped heterogeneously (four or five students per group) with varied language acquisition and ability levels. Once grouped, they count off so that each student has a number. Prepared questions (at different levels of difficulty) are displayed on a transparency or PowerPoint. As the questions are revealed, each group discusses possible answers, finding consensus on one answer. The teacher then spins a spinner and calls out a number from 1–4 or 1–5. If the number is 2, all the students who are number 2 in each group stand up and give their group's answer. Though everyone in the group is responsible for the answer, only one person in each group is chosen to report the group's answer.

While Numbered Heads Together is highly effective, it does take some time to teach the procedures, but once students understand how to participate, the possibilities are endless. Numbered Heads Together can also be used for "finding the one right answer," such as solving math equations. It can be used for answering open-ended questions where each group may have a different answer. It is very effective for standardized test preparation, where students have cards that say a, b, c, or d. The person whose letter is called displays that group's answer and rationale.

SIOP® Connection

Content Objectives:

Students will be able to (SWBAT) . . .

- Come to consensus as a group on a response to a question (or statement) about (a topic).

- Provide a rationale for the group's response to the question about (a topic).

- Evaluate how well prepared they are as a group to answer questions and discuss (the topic).

(continued)

SIOP® Connection *(continued)*

Language Objectives:

Students will be able to (SWBAT) . . .

- In a group, discuss questions and responses related to (the topic).
- Come to consensus about their responses by respectfully agreeing and disagreeing with each other, using the following sentence frames:

   "I disagree with your answer because I believe it should be _____."

   "The correct answer is _____ because _____."

   "I agree you have the correct answer because _____."

Vocabulary-Go-Fish

SIOP® SHELTERED INSTRUCTION OBSERVATION PROTOCOL

COMPONENT: Practice and Application (and Strategies)

(Adapted from Judy Senneff, Long Beach Unified School District)

Grade Levels: K–8

Subject Areas: All

Grouping Configuration: Small groups

Approximate Time Involved: 5–10 minutes for preparation and as much time as desired to play the game.

Materials: Vocabulary cards

Description:

The purpose of Vocabulary-Go-Fish is to increase students' vocabulary in a cooperative setting. Create any number of vocabulary cards; a simple word on one side of the card with a corresponding picture on the other side. More challenging cards might have a word on one side and a definition, synonym, antonym, or sentence on the other. Each group receives a paper bag that holds slips of paper with the vocabulary words on them. The students are numbered within each group, and when the teacher calls a number, the student with that number will Go Fish for a vocabulary word. The teacher then tells the students what response to give for the words they drew (e.g., a synonym, sentence, or definition). The student who has gone fishing reads the word, gives the information, and checks for accuracy by looking on the back of the card. Students' responses may be given orally or in writing.

Older students can be enlisted to create the cards for younger students, and then play Go Fish with them. Beginning English speakers can develop their language proficiency by creating and illustrating cards with vocabulary words, and then play Go Fish with younger students.

In a sheltered 9th grade Literature class, the students played a modified Go Fish game with literary elements and definitions. They had read "The Cask of Amontillado" by Edgar Allen Poe and were engaging in literary analysis with the following terms: Setting, character, narrator, character interaction, irony, symbolism and allegory, figurative language, and imagery. All English learners, the teenagers played Go Fish with as much enthusiasm as you might expect from younger children. The game also provided additional practice and application with the literary elements and their definitions.

SIOP® Connection

Content Objectives:

Students will be able to (SWBAT) . . .

- Match (vocabulary words to their definitions, synonyms, anonyms, etc.).
- Define (vocabulary related to a topic).

(continued)

SIOP® Connection (continued)

Language Objectives:

Students will be able to (SWBAT) . . .

- Provide (definitions, antonyms, synonyms, etc.) for (vocabulary words), using the following sentence frames.

  "_____ is an antonym for _____."

  "_____ is a synonym for _____."

  "_____ is a definition for _____."

- Find their matching cards by using the following sentence frame:

  "My card says _____."

  "What does your card say?"

  "Do you want to trade?"

  "Do we have a match?"

The SIOP® Model: Practice and Application

Lesson Plans

The following lesson plans include the activity Poetry and Patterns (p. 133) although the lessons incorporate all eight of the SIOP® components the emphasis here is on Practice and Application. Students are given an opportunity to creatively practice and apply key vocabulary that are scientific terms. Vocabulary development and academic achievement are strongly related, so sufficient time for students to use academic vocabulary must be provided while ELs are applying their new content and language knowledge in meaningful activities. In the following lessons the teacher uses poetry, specifically Haiku, as a means to practice and apply the scientific terms. Students learn about science as they are reinforcing their language arts skills through reading, writing, listening and speaking.

These lesson plans serve as an example; depending on your grade level and state standards, you can substitute the appropriate resources and content standards. This example demonstrates how to incorporate the Practice and Application component of the SIOP® Model into a lesson plan.

FIGURE 7.11 *Elementary Lesson Plan*

SIOP® Lesson: Metamorphosis   *Grades: 2–4*

Key: SW = Students will; TW = Teacher will; SWBAT = Students will be able to . . . ; HOTS = Higher Order Thinking Skills

Content Standard: Strand 4-Life Science Concept 2-Life Cycles,
PO1: Describe the life cycle of various insects

Key Vocabulary: metamorphosis, larva, chrysalis, pupa, butterfly, & caterpillar	**Visuals/Resources/Supplementary Materials:** Overhead, Post-it ™ chart paper, markers, book *The Hungry Caterpillar* by Eric Carle; previous graphic organizers of Butterfly Life Cycle.
Higher Order Thinking Questions: How would you compare the life cycle of people to that of the butterfly? How are they the same? How might they be different?	

Connections to Prior Knowledge/ Building Background Information:
TW read the story "The Hungry Caterpillar"
As teacher reads the story students will be asked to define the different stages of the caterpillar.
Students will be asked, in their small groups, to review butterfly life cycle graphic organizer previously completed and share one stage and its description.

Content Objectives:	Meaningful Activities:	Review/Assessment:
1. SWBAT choose the operational definition of scientific terms (stages of the butterfly life cycle).	**1.1** TW read the story.	
	1.2 Students will be given a partially completed worksheet of the stages of the butterfly.	
	1.3 SW, as teacher reads, list the definition of each of the scientific terms related to the stages of a butterfly, ex. *larva* and *chrysalis*.	**1.3** Operational definitions of each stage listed in appropriate wording and order.
	1.4 SW, after completing the sheet, be asked to turn to a partner and share one definition.	
	1.5 TW then, on the overhead, share a completed lifecycle with appropriate definitions for students to compare and correct on their sheets if needed.	*(continued)*

FIGURE 7.11 *Elementary Lesson Plan for Practice and Application* (continued)

Language Objectives:		
1. SWBAT use key vocabulary to create a Haiku, defining each word and presenting it to the group.	**1.1** TW define what is meant by Haiku and give two examples using the key vocabulary word, *metamorphosis,* one correct and one incorrect. For example: *Metamorphosis* *Any change of "u"* *In appearances*	
	1.2 SW determine if the example is correct or incorrect (thumbs up for yes, thumbs down for no).	**1.2** Active response/elaborate why or why not.
	1.3 SW, in small groups, be assigned one key vocabulary word and asked to write two Haikus defining the term, using a true example and a false example.	**1.3** Completed Haikus: one true and one false.
	1.4 SW in their groups present their Haikus to the whole group. The group will vote with thumbs up if they believe the Haiku is correct or thumbs-down if it is incorrect.	**1.4** Active responses with thumbs up and down. For incorrect, SW make suggestions on how to make it correct.

Wrap-up: Cloze sentences summarizing key vocabulary.
The _____ of a butterfly has _____ stages. The first stage is a _____. The next stage, _____ occurs when the _____ _____. The _____ then becomes a _____. And finally, there is the _____.

Source: Lesson plan created by Melissa Castillo and Nicole Teyechea. Lesson content created by Melissa Castillo.

FIGURE 7.12 *Secondary Lesson Plan for Practice and Application*

SIOP® *Lesson: Atomic Particles*   Grade: 9

Content Standard: Strand 5: Physical Science:
Concept 1: Structure and Properties of Matter Understand Physical, chemical and atomic properties of matter.
PO 6: Describe the features and components of the atom: Matter, Mass, Protons, Neutrons and Electrons

Key Vocabulary: matter, mass, atom, proton, neutron and electrons **Higher Order Thinking Questions:** How can a scientist guess what atoms look like? What causes the particles of an atom to stay together?	**Visuals/ Resources/Supplementary Materials:** Introduction to Atoms handout (after looking at the websites a handout can be easily written); websites: www.thetech.org/atomtour & www.education.jlab.org/atomtour; computer, projector to run web pages; screen; chart paper and markers; index cards

Connections to Prior Knowledge/ Building Background Information:
TW ask students the following questions:
What do you think everything is made of?
Are people, animals, and objects made of the same thing? Yes or no? Explain.
SW do a quick-write answering the questions on an index card. SW turn to a partner and share their responses.

FIGURE 7.12 *Secondary Lesson Plan for Practice and Application* *(continued)*

Content Objectives:	Meaningful Activities:	Review/Assessment:
1. SW demonstrate knowledge of key vocabulary by choosing the operational definition of scientific terms.	1.1 SW view the first webpage listed above. 1.2 TW stop and ask a few questions about what is being observed, partially completing a transparency of the intro to Atoms handout.	
	1.3 SW view the second web page and in pairs define the key vocabulary words listed on the handout and finish answering questions.	1.3 Operational definition of all key vocabulary listed.
	1.4 TW ask students to share answers and definitions for vocabulary words, completing the transparency with the appropriate responses for students to compare and correct on their sheets if needed.	
Language Objectives:		
1. SW use key vocabulary to create a Haiku giving an example defining the word and presenting to the group.	1.1 TW explain what a Haiku is and give examples. 1.2 TW use one key vocabulary word as an example: *Matter will* *Sometimes weigh a lot* *Give it space*	
	1.3 SW determine if the example is correct or incorrect (thumbs up for yes, thumbs down for no) and share in small groups why.	1.3 Active response/elaborate why or why not.
	1.4 SW, in small groups, be assigned one key vocabulary word and asked to write a Haiku using a true example of what the word means and include an illustrated example.	1.4 Completed Haiku with appropriate example.
	1.5 SW, in their groups, present their Haikus to the whole group.	

Wrap-up: Outcome Sentences

I thought . . .

I wonder . . .

I learned . . .

Each student will write an outcome sentence and share it with their small group.

SW count off in their groups, TW call out a number, Student from each of the group with that number will stand and share.

Source: Lesson plan created by Melissa Castillo and Nicole Teyechea. Lesson content created by Melissa Castillo.

chapter 8

Lesson Delivery

Overview of the Lesson Delivery Component

Have you ever written a fabulous lesson plan—with all the bells and whistles you could think of—but when you taught the lesson, it went far differently than you had planned? The Lesson Delivery component of the SIOP® Model focuses on this common problem. It's one thing to *write* the lesson and another to *deliver* it effectively. Because explicit content and language objectives guide the development of all SIOP® lessons, the subsequent instruction must clearly support these objectives. Consider the following content and language objectives:

- *Content Objective:* Students will be able to demonstrate knowledge of the life cycle of amphibians (the frog) by illustrating and labeling the stages.
- *Language Objective:* Students will be able to analyze the life cycle of amphibians (the frog) by writing a summary from cloze sentences.

In order for students to meet these two objectives, the teacher must explicitly teach the stages of the life cycle of amphibians (the frog), plan meaningful activities to provide practice and application with these life cycle stages, and assess the extent to which students know and can label the stages. Everything students do during this lesson prepares them to meet the content and language objectives. This requires very high student engagement (no wasted instructional time), with appropriate pacing so that all students have a reasonable expectation of meeting the objectives. In all teaching, Lesson Delivery is where the rubber meets the road.

The Lesson Delivery component includes the following features:

23. Content objectives clearly supported by lesson delivery.
24. Language objectives clearly supported by lesson delivery.
25. Students engaged approximately 90% to 100% of the period.
26. Pacing of the lesson appropriate to the students' ability level.

Ideas and Activities for Implementing Lesson Delivery

Stand Up–Sit Down[*]

[*]similar to Take a Stand

SIOP® SHELTERED INSTRUCTION OBSERVATION PROTOCOL | **COMPONENT:** Lesson Delivery (and Review/Assessment)

Grade Levels: K–12
Subject Levels: All
Grouping Configurations: Small groups or whole class
Approximate Time Involved: 5–15 minutes depending on number of questions posed
Materials: None

Description:

Stand Up–Sit Down gives students the opportunity to respond to true/false statements through movement as the teacher monitors student comprehension during lesson delivery. The teacher makes a statement about the content being taught and students must decide if it is true or false (or accurate/inaccurate). If a student decides the statement is true, he or she stands up. If the student believes the statement is false, he or she remains seated. The teacher calls on two or three students who hold differing views and each is asked to explain his or her rationale for standing or sitting. After a student provides a reason for his or her answer, the other students may change their minds and either join the group that is standing, or join those who are sitting. The students' explanations help others to rethink which is the most reasonable or correct/incorrect answer to the question, and the teacher can take advantage of the teachable moment. Stand Up–Sit Down is a quick assessment of comprehension during lesson delivery, while allowing students to clarify their own understanding. Older students can create their own true/false (or correct/incorrect) statements related to a subject area, and "test" their peers' reactions to the statements.

> ## ⟋ SIOP® Connection
>
> **Content Objective:**
> Students will be able to (SWBAT) . . .
>
> - Determine if statements made about (a topic) are true or false, and provide a rationale for their decisions.
>
> *(continued)*

SIOP® Connection (continued)

Language Objective:

Students will be able to (SWBAT) . . .

- State their reasons for why they believe a statement about (a topic) is true or false by using the following sentence frames:

  "I believe that statement is true because _____."

  "I believe that statement if false because _____."

Heading into Questions

COMPONENT: Lesson Delivery (and Strategies)

(Adapted from Angie Medina, Long Beach Unified School District)

Grade Levels: 1–12
Subject Levels: All
Grouping Configurations: Individual, partners, small groups, or whole class
Approximate Time Involved: 5–30 minutes depending on grouping configuration
Materials: Text for students to read

Description:

As a teacher delivers a lesson, it is criticial that students have a purpose for reading so they see the path they are to follow. Questions provide ELs with that purpose. Guide students to look at the bold headings to predict the types of questions that may be asked about the information in the text. Initially this activity should be modeled for the entire class; with the text copied on transparencies, demonstrate how to turn the headings and subheadings in a chapter into questions using words such as *who, what, where, when, why,* and *how.* These questions become the focus and purpose for the subsequent reading. Students use them to monitor their comprehension throughout the text. After frequent opportunities to practice with the teacher's guidance, students can create the questions individually, in partners, and in small groups. No matter how students are grouped, they can split up the task, turning each heading into a question, writing the questions, and presenting them to the rest of the class. The questions and answers can be written on chart paper with the answers filled in during the lesson delivery.

SIOP® Connection

Content Objective:

Students will be able to (SWBAT) . . .

- Turn chapter headings into key questions and then answer the questions after reading about (a topic).

Language Objective:

Students will be able to (SWBAT) . . .

- Use question words (*who, what, where, when, why, how*) to turn headings into questions.

Chunk and Chew

SIOP® SHELTERED INSTRUCTION OBSERVATION PROTOCOL **COMPONENT:** Lesson Delivery

(Jo Gusman, New Horizons in Education, Inc.)

Grade Levels: All
Subject Levels: All
Grouping Configurations: Individual, partners, small groups, or whole class
Approximate Time Involved: Duration of lesson
Materials: None

Description:

Chunk and Chew ensures that students are not inundated with input from the teacher without being given appropriate time to process information. By following the Chunk and Chew strategy, teachers deliver their lessons is small "chunks" giving students time to "chew" the information either individually, with partners, or in small groups. Follow this simple rule: For every 10 minutes of teacher input, students should be given 2 minutes to process the information. (This is known as 10 and 2). Time frames vary and should be adjusted according to language proficiency and grade level of the students. When students are aware of the strategy of the Chunk and Chew technique, they will anticipate the processing time and let the teacher know when they have reached their limit on input.

🔎 SIOP® Connection

This particular activity for Lesson Delivery does not lend itself to specific content or language objectives; it is information for the teacher to use during a lesson.

Magic Buttons

SIOP® COMPONENT: Lesson Delivery

(Adapted by Angie Medina, Long Beach Unified School District)

Grade Levels: K–4
Subject Levels: All
Grouping Configurations: Individuals, or partners
Approximate Time Involved: 1 minute
Materials: Handout with Magic Buttons (see Figures 8.1 and 8.2)

Description:

Magic Buttons allows students think-time during a lesson. Each student is given two buttons: an "I'm thinking!" button and an "I got it!" button. After the teacher poses a question, the students' hands should remain on the "I'm thinking" button until they have had sufficient time to process the information. When they are ready to respond, students should move their hands to the "I got it!" button to show that their thinking is complete. This technique allows the teacher to monitor student think-time to ensure that adequate time is given to process the information. Students see the importance of the thinking process itself, rather than simply validating the correct answer.

Once the majority of class members have their hands on the "I got it!" button, the teacher can move the discussion to partners, small groups, or whole class. Another version of Magic Buttons is to give students an opportunity to agree or disagree non-verbally through the pressing of a button.

🔭 SIOP® Connection

Content Objective:

Students will be able to (SWBAT) . . .

- Monitor their own thinking and processing about (a topic) by deciding (after think-time) when they are ready to respond to a teacher's questions.

Language Objective:

Students will be able to (SWBAT) . . .

- Orally explain their responses to teacher questions and how they arrived at them.

FIGURE 8.1 *Magic Buttons #1*

Source: © 2006 Pearson Achievement Solutions, a division of Pearson Education. All rights reserved.

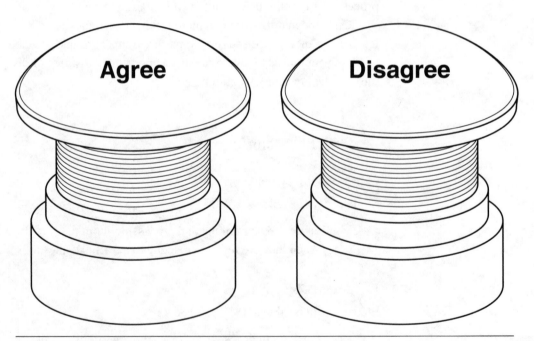

FIGURE 8.2 *Magic Buttons #2*

Source: © 2006 Pearson Achievement Solutions, a division of Pearson Education. All rights reserved.

Procedural Knowledge

COMPONENT: Lesson Delivery (and Strategies)

(Lipson & Wixson, 2003)

Grade Levels: All
Subject Levels: All
Grouping Configurations: Whole class
Approximate Time Involved: 15–20 minutes
Materials: None

Description:

Procedural Knowledge allows students to become familiar with the procedural steps of a particular learning or instructional strategy. Learning strategies are those acquired behaviors (such as routinely predicting and previewing) learners use to make sense of new information; they "reside" in the learner's head. Instructional strategies are those techniques, methods, and approaches teachers use to help students acquire necessary learning behaviors (such as the ideas presented in this book).

When introducing a new learning or instructional strategy (during lesson delivery), it is important to remember that students need time to understand the procedural steps before they attempt to connect the strategy to content. The first time students use a strategy, it is helpful if the topic is something very familiar to them (e.g., favorite foods or hobbies). This ensures that the procedures will be learned and students will not be sidetracked by unfamiliar content. Once students understand the procedure, they can use the strategy in connection with the content. By frequently reinforcing a learning or instructional strategy, the procedure becomes secondary and students begin to tackle content with ease. It is best to implement one strategy at a time, however, so that students become familiar with the procedure. Repeating helps students "own" it so that they can use it again and again with very little teacher instruction.

Marge Lipson and Karen Wixson (2008) suggest that teachers also emphasize Declarative Knowledge (what the strategy is) and Conditional Knowledge (under what conditions or circumstances one might need to employ the strategy). When students follow the procedural steps without understanding what kind of strategic thinking they're using, the chance of their internalizing the strategy is minimal at best.

SIOP® Connection

This particular idea does not lend itself to specific content or language objectives; it is information for the teacher to use when teaching a lesson.

Response Cards

COMPONENT: Lesson Delivery (and Review/Assessment)

Grade Levels: All
Subject Levels: All
Grouping Configurations: Individual, partners, small groups
Approximate Time Involved: 5 minutes
Materials: Response cards

Description:

Although we recommend that English learners have multiple opportunities to speak, there are times, especially in the beginning stages of learning English, when students may be more comfortable responding nonverbally. Response Cards allow students to respond to questions that have an answer of 1–4 or a–d. Each student is given a sheet of paper with the numbers 1–4 on one side and the letters a–d on the other; the students fold the paper in fourths so that only one number or letter is showing at a time. The teacher reads a question either from the overhead, chart, text, or test practice book, than reads the four possible choices. The students respond by folding the Response Card to show the number or letter which corresponds with the answer they believe to be true. As students become more proficient with Response Cards, they can read both the questions and the possible answer choices. This activity can be modified by giving one Response Card to each set of partners or small group.

Response Cards can also be made with 2″ × 6″ strips of tagboard (see Figure 8.3). On one side of the Card, write (vertically) the numbers 0, 1, 2, 3, 4. The zero indicates "I don't know" or "I'm not sure." Students place their index fingers on the pertinent number in response to a question with multiple choice possibilities. These Response Cards can fulfill two purposes if "Agree" and "Disagree" are written at the top and bottom of the other side of the card; when students are asked a question about which they can agree or disagree, they hold up the appropriate response. The most beneficial aspect of Response Cards is that they provide the teacher with immediate feedback about how well students comprehend the lesson content.

For standardized test preparation, numbers can be replaced by the letters a, b, c, d.

> ### SIOP® Connection
>
> This particular activity for Lesson Delivery does not lend itself to specific content or language objectives; as it is information for the teacher to use when planning the delivery of a lesson.

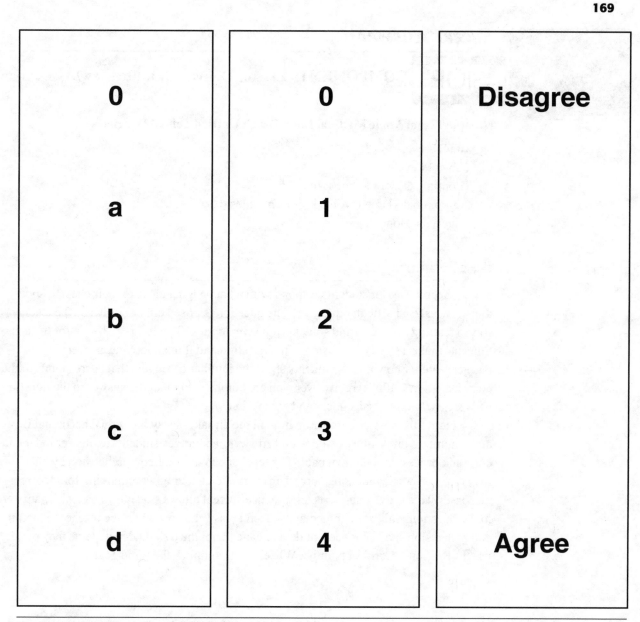

FIGURE 8.3 *Response Cards*

Secret Answer

SIOP® | **COMPONENT:** Lesson Delivery (and Review/Assessment)

(Adapted from Angie Medina, Long Beach Unified School District)

Grade Levels: K–8
Subject Levels: All
Grouping Configurations: Individual
Approximate Time Involved: 2–15 minutes
Materials: None

Description:

During Secret Answer students respond with a hand signal close to their chest to show their answer to a particular question. The question is posed either orally (by the teacher) or from a reading (in a text) and students are given options labeled 1, 2, 3, or 4 for the answer. Students make a fist as they listen to the question and think about the answer. On the teacher's cue ("Show me!"), students show the number of fingers that corresponds to the correct answer. With Secret Answer, you are emphasizing that the answer to the question is between each individual student and the teacher.

Holding the answer number up high in the air takes away individual accountability and minimizes think-time, while Secret Answer encourages students to answer independently and process at their own pace. The teacher can monitor comprehension by checking the Secret Answers, validating correct answers and encouraging rethinking for incorrect responses. This activity supports test practice since it allows students to have their answers to test questions validated immediately. Secret Answer also enables the teacher to monitor comprehension and keeps each student engaged with the task. Older students may prefer to use the Response Cards or Number Wheels to accomplish the same goal.

SIOP® Connection

This particular activity for Lesson Delivery does not lend itself to specific content or language objectives; it is information for the teacher to use when planning the delivery of a lesson.

Take Your Corners

COMPONENT: Lesson Delivery
(and Practice Application)

(Adapted from Kagan, 1994)

Grade Levels: 2–12
Subject Levels: All
Grouping Configurations: Whole class
Approximate Time Involved: 20–40 minutes
Materials: Paper labels for the four corners of the room; index cards

Description:

Take Your Corners allows students to show their opinion in a non-threatening way through physical movement. Each corner of the room is labeled with a category or opinion. Students do a quick-draw (illustration) on an index card to represent their opinion, mixing around the room to share their quick-draw with others until the teacher calls "Freeze." At this point the students are encouraged to point to the corner that best corresponds to their opinion. When the teacher calls, "Go," students walk to their respective corners and share their opinions with one another. The teacher roams from corner to corner to monitor understanding and take advantage of teachable moments. As the students separate into their corners, the instruction becomes whole-class as students look to the teacher for clarification, and debate their opinions against students in other corners. This activity works well at the beginning of instruction, during lesson delivery, and as closure to a lesson.

SIOP® Connection

Content Objective:

Students will be able to (SWBAT) . . .

- Choose one of four opinions (about a topic, e.g., one of four presidents who made the most meaningful contributions to American society) and defend their opinions based on the information they have acquired through instruction research.

Language Objectives:

Students will be able to (SWBAT) . . .

- State their opinions while showing respect for others' ideas by using the following sentence frames:

    "I believe_____."

    "I feel_____."

    "My opinion is_____."

(continued)

SIOP® Connection (continued)

● Disagree with other students while showing respect for their opinions by using the following sentence frames:

"I disagree with that statement about _____ because _____."

"I understand your opinion, but _____."

"Have you ever thought of _____?"

What Do You Know?

SIOP® OBSERVATION PROTOCOL | **COMPONENT:** Lesson Delivery (and Preparation)

Grade Levels: K–12
Subject Levels: All
Grouping Configurations: Small groups or whole class
Approximate Time Involved: 5–15 minutes (depending on group discussion)
Materials: Supplemental materials, e.g., photos, illustrations, and realia

Description:

How many times have you been teaching a lesson that seems to be going well until you ask students some questions like "What do you know about (the topic)?" or "What can you tell me about that?" With English learners, it's not surprising that the response is sometimes limited (a few words), one sentence, or perhaps a blank stare. An English learner's inability to answer may not indicate a lack of comprehension, but rather a lack of connection to the topic, as well as difficulty expressing in English what is known about the topic.

In contrast, a student will have more to connect with when the teacher poses a question while showing photos, illustrations, and/or realia related directly to the topic under discussion. This scaffolding allows a more accurate assessment of understanding and facilitates comprehension. It also provides students with tangible, familiar items which they can describe and talk about; abstract concepts thus become concrete. Photos and illustrations can come from a textbook, the Internet, or other resources, copied to a transparency, or enlarged for the whole class to view. Realia, artifacts and real-life materials related to the content may be shared by teacher and students alike. When English learners have the ability to see something at the same time they hear about it, their chances for understanding the topic are enhanced.

> ### 🧭 SIOP® Connection
>
> This particular activity for Lesson Delivery does not lend itself to specific content or language objectives; it is information for the teacher to use when planning the delivery of a lesson.

Stop that Video-DVD

SIOP® COMPONENT: Lesson Delivery (and Preparation)

(Adapted from Long Beach Unified School Distric)

Grade Levels: All   Subject Levels: All   Grouping Configurations: Whole class
Approximate Time Involved: 30–60 minutes (depending on grade level and the length
of the video)   Materials: A video, note-taking worksheet or outline

Description:

English learners (and others) while watching a content-related video may talk throughout, be asked to quiet down, and have nothing to share related to the content at the close of the video. This problem may result from inadequate processing time and be resolved by using the technique, Stop That Video-DVD.

During this activity, the teacher stops the video at key points, allowing students time to process the information individually, either in their heads or on paper. English learners particularly benefit from using a note-taking sheet that outlines key points or questions to be answered in the video. Once students process information independently, they can share and clarify it with a partner.

This technique allows the teacher to check for understanding throughout the course of the video and address any misconceptions. If a student chooses to process the information with another student in their primary language, this may further enhance comprehension.

SIOP® Connection

Content Objective:

Students will be able to (SWBAT) . . .

- Stop periodically while viewing a video-DVD on (a topic) and summarize what has just been seen.

Language Objective:

Students will be able to (SWBAT) . . .

- Use sequence words (e.g., *in the beginning, then, next, before, after, finally,* etc.) to summarize what they have seen in a video-DVD (on a topic).

The SIOP® Model: Lesson Delivery

Lesson Plans

Note: The Lesson Delivery component brings written lesson plans to life in the classroom. It isn't possible to create a lesson with a focus on Lesson Delivery—the entire lesson is all about its delivery! There are no lesson plans therefore, for this component of the SIOP® Model.

chapter 9

Review and Assessment

Overview of the Review and Assessment Component

Although the component of Review and Assessment is the eighth on the SIOP® protocol, the process of reviewing and assessing student understanding is ongoing and continuous. Best practice—and common sense—dictate that we assess students before, during, and after lessons, and that assessment findings guide lesson design and instruction.

It is beyond the scope of this book to include a wide variety of assessment instruments for diagnosing reading and writing abilities, language proficiency, and general achievement. (For more in-depth information on assessment, diagnosis, and evaluation see the Lipson and Wixson, 2008, reference at the end of this book, or other texts devoted to the topic). Results of various assessments, some administered by the classroom teacher and others by specialists, add to the informal day-to-day gathering of information about student progress.

The ideas and activities in this chapter are intended to provide teachers with additional insight into how English learners demonstrate their knowledge and application of key vocabulary and concepts. They provide opportunities for teachers to give specific, focused, academic feedback—not just "very good" or "nice job"—but the type of feedback students can use to self-assess their progress meeting content and language objectives. This feedback might include comments such as: "It's great to see you working together as a team! You're listening well to each other and making sure everyone is getting it!" "I noticed that you said . . . . . .; could you tell me more about that?" "I can see you understand this because you just used today's vocabulary words. That tells me that you understand their meanings!" The more specific and academic our feedback to English learners, the more they are able to self-monitor and adjust.

The Review and Assessment component includes the following features:

27. Comprehensive review of key vocabulary.

28. Comprehensive review of key content concepts.

29. Regular feedback provided to students on their output (e.g., language, content, work).

30. Assessment of student comprehension and learning of all lesson objectives (e.g., spot checking, group response) throughout the lesson.

Ideas and Activities for Review and Assessment

Share Bear

SIOP® | **COMPONENT:** Review/Assessment

(Adapted from Angie Medina, Long Beach Unified School District)

Grade Levels: K–3
Subject Areas: All
Grouping Configuration: Small groups
Approximate Time Involved: 5–10 minutes for the discussion (depending on the teacher's purposes)
Materials: A stuffed bear for each table group

Description:

Share Bear encourages all students in a group to engage in higher level thinking, participate, and wait their turn. There is one Share Bear (a stuffed animal) at each table. After the teacher poses an open ended question (e.g., "How did you feel when _____?" "Why did the _____?" "What do you remember about _____?" "How would you _____?"), one student at each table takes the Share Bear, and gives his or her response to the question, passing the Share Bear to the next student who then gives his or her response. This continues until each student has shared or had multiple turns. If, while walking around the room, a teacher hears language errors (e.g., "The boy *go* because . . . "), the teacher may interject (e.g., "Right, the boy *went* because . . . ").

SIOP® Connection

Content Objective:

Students will be able to (SWBAT) . . .

- Take turns answering questions, discussing, and explaining information about (a topic).

Language Objective:

Students will be able to (SWBAT) . . .

- Use the following sentence frames:

    "I think that _____."

    "I believe that _____ because _____."

Simultaneous Round Table

COMPONENT: Review/Assessment

(Kagan, 1994)

Grade Levels: All
Grouping Configuration: Small groups
Approximate Time Involved: About 10 minutes
Materials: Paper and pencils

Description:

Simultaneous Round Table encourages students to work with each other as they review. Each student at the table group (four or five students) is given a paper and a pencil. The papers are labeled with a team number (rather than students' own names) because the paper will be passed around the group. The teacher poses a question with multiple short answers. Students are given two minutes to respond to the question and then they pass the papers to each group member four or five times. Each time the paper is passed to a student, he or she must read what is already on the list and then add additional ideas. Students may write an answer they have seen on another piece of paper or create a new answer. This allows students to review individually, yet with the support of their team members.

For example, through the activity of Simultaneous Round Table, students review what they learned about pioneers and wagon trains by reading their peers' thoughts and adding their own ideas. The lists circulate around the table until complete, and each student then reads his or her list to the rest of the team. When the teams report, the teacher can generate one class list of information about the pioneers' wagon trains.

SIOP® Connection

Content Objective:

Students will be able to (SWBAT) . . .

- Generate answers to questions about (a topic), and respond to the comments of peers on a group list.

Language Objective:

Students will be able to (SWBAT) . . .

- Write their ideas about (the topic) on the group list.
- Read and discuss with group members the listed ideas.

Number 1–3 For Self-Assessment of Objectives

COMPONENT: Review/Assessment
(Building Background)

Grade Levels: K–12
Subject Areas: All
Grouping Configuration: Whole class
Approximate Time Involved: 3–5 minutes
Materials: None

Description:

It's one thing for the teacher to assess student progress toward meeting objectives; it's something entirely different for students to assess their own progress and understandings. This is a quick and easy way for students to self-assess the degree to which they think they have met a lesson's content and language objectives. At the end of the lesson, review the objectives with the students and ask them to indicate with one, two, or three fingers how well they think they met them:

> 1 = I didn't (or can't) meet (or do) the objective.
>
> 2 = I didn't (or can't) meet (or do) the objective, but I made progress toward meeting it.
>
> 3 = I fully met (or can do) the objective.

Depending on how students indicate their understanding of a lesson's key concepts (objectives), the teacher can reteach, provide additional modeling, group students for further instruction and practice, and so forth. Self-assessments that are directly related to a lesson's content and language objectives are far more informative than the typical students' "yeah" or "no" or "sorta" comments that arise when teachers ask whether the lesson's objectives have been met.

SIOP® Connection

This particular idea does not lend itself to specific content or language objectives; it is information for the teacher to use when planning assessment of a lesson's content and language objectives.

Self-Assessment Rubrics

 **COMPONENT:** Review/Assessment

Grade Levels: 1–12
Subject Areas: All
Grouping Configuration: Individual
Approximate Time Involved: 5–10 minutes (depending on age/grade level)
Materials: A copy of the rubric for each student

Description:

One way for students to self-assess is to provide them with Self-Assessment Rubrics. In grades K–2, these may be as simple as smiley faces, question marks, and sad faces (☺ ? ☹). After reading a statement about the lesson, the children mark (with an X) the symbol that most closely corresponds to their own feelings. Older students can circle or mark the number on the rubric that best matches how they perceive their understandings (0 = I don't understand; 1 = I think I understand; 2 = I understand but I still have questions; 3 = I understand but I can't really explain (the concepts) to others; 4 = I understand and can explain (the concepts) to others.

🔍 SIOP® Connection

This particular idea does not lend itself to specific content or language objectives; it is information for the teacher to use when planning assessment of a lesson's content and language objectives.

Mix and Match with Essay Direction Words

SIOP® **COMPONENT:** Review/Assessment

Grade Levels: 4–12 (depending on English proficiency of students)
Subject Areas: All   Grouping Configuration: Whole class Approximate Time
Involved: About 10–15 minutes   Materials: Index cards with direction words on
half and their definitions on the other half

Description:

With the National Assessment of Educational Progress (NAEP) and state tests now requiring that students write essays, it is important that teachers assist English learners in understanding the academic language inherent in essay writing. Students will learn the
meanings of direction words for writing essays by practicing writing; however, English
learners (and perhaps other students) may not know the meanings of the words that direct
them to the type of writing they are expected to do.

Mix and Match (similar to Idiom Match Up) is a great way to review the meanings of
any vocabulary words, including those that provide directions for writing; essays. (Prior to
reviewing with Mix and Match, terms should be explicitly taught and modeled, with
specific examples, in writing). Write (or have students write) a term on half of the index
cards; write a matching definition for each term on the other cards. Students randomly
draw a term or definition. They then try to find their match with one student asking: "I
have (term). What do you have?" The second student responds, "I have (definition)." If
they match, they move to the outside of the group. Cards can be shuffled and re-dealt for
another round of Mix and Match once the initial matches have been made. When all
matches have been completed, partners read their matching terms and definitions aloud.
Mix and Match can be played as frequently as necessary.

Examples of the academic language necessary for writing effective essays include:

- *Analyze:* Examine critically to show essential features
- *Criticize:* Point out strong and weak points (also "evaluate")
- *Compare:* Show differences and similarities between two or more things
- *Contrast:* Compare to show differences only
- *Define:* Give a clear, detailed, and precise meaning *(who* or *what;* never *when* or *where)*
- *Describe:* List physical characteristics; could also mean to *discuss, explain, identify,*
  or *give account of*
- *Discuss:* Comment on topic; present essentials and their relationships
- *Elaborate:* Develop theme or idea in greater detail
- *Evaluate:* Appraise carefully, giving positive and negative aspects *(critique)*
- *Explain:* Clarify and interpret details of the problem, theory, etc.; present a step-by-
  step account of or analysis *(how* and *why)*
- *Illustrate:* Explain or clarify by giving clear, pertinent examples (give examples of)
- *List:* Set down under each other a series of facts, names, dates, etc.; write a series of
  numbered items
- *Outline:* Organize facts by arranging them in a series of headings and subheadings
  to show relationships
- *Prove:* List all logical arguments supporting the statements
- *Summarize:* Present concisely all main points

Find Someone Who

COMPONENT: Review/Assessment
(Building Background)

(Kagan, 1994)

Grade Levels: 2–12
Subject Areas: All
Grouping Configuration: Whole class
Approximate Time Involved: About 10–15 minutes
Materials: Review sheet for each student

Description:

Find Someone Who involves students helping each other review previously taught information. Students are given a review sheet and circulate around the room to find help in answering the questions on the sheet. They approach each other and ask a question; if a student knows the answer, he tells it and the other student writes it on his review sheet. The student who gave the information signs or initials next to the answer. Each student may give information to no more than one question on another student's paper. After a given time students take their seats and the teacher facilitates a review of the answers so students can check their papers for accuracy.

SIOP® Connection

Content Objectives:

Students will be able to (SWBAT) . . .

- Ask and answer questions about (a topic).
- Decide if other students' answers are correct or incorrect.

Language Objectives:

Students will be able to (SWBAT) . . .

- Read questions to other students.
- Listen to another student's answer to a question and write that response, if it is deemed correct, on the review sheet.
- Orally tell a correct answer to a question posed by another student.

Numbered Heads Together with a Review Sheet

SIOP® | **COMPONENT:** Review/Assessment

SHELTERED INSTRUCTION
OBSERVATION PROTOCOL

(Adapted from Kagan, 1994)

Grade Levels: 3–12
Subject Areas: All
Grouping Configuration: Small groups
Approximate Time Involved: About 5 minutes
Materials: Review sheet and pencil for each student

Description:

Numbered Heads Together with a Review Sheet, offers peer support for review of unit content. Each student is given a review sheet and a pencil. The teacher reads the first question aloud to students. In a small group, students put their heads together to come to a consensus on the answer; they can use the text or other resources to determine their group answer (e.g., instruments for a unit on measurement). The teacher calls a number and students from each table with that number stand to answer for that group. If a student's answer is incorrect, the teacher may respond, "I can see how your team might think that, but the answer actually is . . . " Once the correct answer is determined, the students write it on their review sheet. The process continues through all of the questions and students review, using listening, speaking, reading, and writing, by completing the tasks with group support.

SIOP® Connection

Content Objective:

Students will be able to (SWBAT) . . .

- Work in a group to review information about (a topic).

Language Objective:

Students will be able to (SWBAT) . . .

- Listen to questions, generate answers in writing, and orally report the answers to class members.

Sign In, Please

COMPONENT: Review/Assessment

Grade Levels: All
Subject Areas: All
Grouping Configuration: Individual
Approximate Time Involved: 5 minutes (depending on the teacher)
Materials: None

Description:

Sign In, Please assesses students' understanding of lesson content. This instructional technique can be used throughout a lesson. When the teacher makes a statement and asks if it is true or false. The students respond with hand signs for true or false: The sign for T (true) is a fist with the thumb protruding between the index and middle finger. The sign for F (false) is the middle, ring, and little finger extended with the thumb holding the fingernail of the index finger flat to the palm. When the teacher sees students with the incorrect response she can explain why the statement is true or false, or ask students to explain their rationale.

SIOP® Connection

Content Objective:

Student will be able to (SWBAT) . . .

- Determine whether a statement is true or false and indicate their response using sign language.

Language Objective:

Students will be able to (SWBAT) . . .

- Listen carefully to statements before determining if they are true or false.

Response Boards

COMPONENT: Review/Assessment

Grade Level: 1–12
Subject Areas: All
Grouping Configuration: Individual, partners, small groups
Approximate Time Involved: 5–10 minutes
Materials: Response boards and marking pens

Description:

Response Boards give the teacher a chance to assess whether students have grasped the fundamentals of a lesson before moving on. Each student, pair, or table group is given a response board. The teacher poses a problem or question for the students to answer. While students are working in pairs or small groups, a designated student writes and displays the response board after conferencing with the others. The teacher can see if the class is ready to progress to the next point.

There are a variety of ways to create response boards: laminated file folders, or tag board (used with vis-à-vis markers or crayon), white boards (inexpensively made with bathroom tile board available at home improvement/lumber stores), chalkboards, or paper and pencil. A response board might also consist of graphics or illustrations related to the content, which the students may point to for their responses.

SIOP® Connection

This particular activity for Review and Assessment does not lend itself to specific content or language objectives; it is information for the teacher to use when planning the review of a lesson.

Find the Fib

SIOP® | **COMPONENT:** Review/Assessment

(Adapted from Kagan, 1994)

Grade Levels: All
Subject Areas: All
Grouping Configuration: Individual, partners, small groups
Approximate Time Involved: 10 minutes if the teacher makes the statements; 15 minutes for the students to write the statements and then as much time as the teacher feels necessary to find the fibs.
Materials: Three fib cards for each student or group

Description:

Find the Fib allows teachers to assess understanding of content, while students are supported in decision-making by their peers. Students work in pairs or small groups, and each has a set of three cards that say: "1 is the fib;" "2 is the fib;" "3 is the fib." The teacher poses three statements, one false and two true; students may also write their own statements, one false and two true. The students then decide independently, with their partner, or in their small group which one is false (the fib). On a signal from the teacher, students show their cards at the same time. If a student has the wrong answer, the teacher asks other students to explain which word or phrase in the fib makes it false. The teacher can also encourage the class to explain which word or phrase in the true statements makes them true.

SIOP® Connection

Content Objective:

Students will be able to (SWBAT) . . .

- Determine whether statements about (a topic) are true or false.

Language Objectives:

Students will be able to (SWBAT) . . .

- Listen to statements about (a topic) orally presented by the teacher.
- Discuss with group members true and false statements about (a topic).
- Write true and false statements about (a topic).

The SIOP® Model: Review and Assessment

Lesson Plans

The following lesson plans include the activity, Piece O'Pizza, p. 148. While the lessons incorporate all eight SIOP® components, the emphasis here is on Review and Assessment. Students are preparing to study the Civil War, so the teacher previews some key vocabulary that was "everyday talk" during the War, especially during the Battle of Gettysburg. The words, considered slang during this time period, will be those that students will encounter during subsequent lessons in the unit.

These activities were selected so that students can apply their content and vocabulary knowledge. In the high school lesson, students are expected to access several websites to locate the slang words and phrases, and are then to use them in context. The elementary students will use a website available through the National Park Service, (www.nps.gov/archive/gett/getteducation/bcast04/04activities/activity05.htm) to find Civil War slang words and create picture books to illustrate the words' meanings. The Piece O' Pizza activity ensures that as students learn about the Civil War they apply vocabulary and content concepts; they must read, write, listen and speak. During these activities, the teacher has many opportunities to observe, provide feedback, and assess student understanding and language use.

Keep in mind these lesson plans serve as examples; depending on your grade level and state standards, you can substitute the appropriate text or Internet websites and content standards. This example is intended to demonstrate how to incorporate the Review and Assessment component of the SIOP® Model into a lesson plan.

FIGURE 9.1 *Elementary Lesson Plan for Review and Assessment*

Key: SW = Students will; TW = Teacher will; SWBAT = Students will be able to . . . ; HOTS = Higher Order Thinking Skills

SIOP® Lesson: Civil War Slang	*Grade: 5*

Content Standards: Life and times during the Civil War; Major battles of the Civil War

Key Vocabulary: Civil War, Battle of Gettysburg, slang, phrase, context **HOTS:** Where do you think slang words and phrases come from? Do you think words and phrases that we use today might change in the future, and if so why? Why do the Civil War slang words seem so strange to us today?	**Visuals/ Resources:** Computers and Internet access, Chart paper, markers; "Read-Aloud Plays: Civil War" (grades 4–8) by Timothy Nolan

Connections to Prior Knowledge/Building Background:

TW ask students to brainstorm in a small group as many slang words or phrases they know and use.
TW records these on chart paper;
SW discuss which are "kids' words" and which are "adult or everyone's words/phrases;" mark with 1 or 2;

Content Objectives:	**Meaningful Activities:**	**Review/Assessment:**
1. SWBAT identify slang words and phrases in a play about the Civil War.	1.1 TW assign parts in play, give 5 min. for oral practice, and SW read a play aloud while looking for any possible slang words/phrases.	1.1 Teacher observation and questioning during read-aloud

(continued)

FIGURE 9.1 *Elementary Lesson Plan for Review and Assessment* *(continued)*

2. SWBAT demonstrate knowledge of current slang and Civil War (CW) slang/key vocabulary by identifying words/phrases and their meanings.	**2.1** TW introduces CW slang words, for example: *bread basket, fit to be tied, pepperbox, horse sense, hunkey dorey, greenhorn;* explain to students what is meant by *slang.* **2.2** TW ask students if they believe these words are still used today; if not what might be a word that means the same? **2.3** SW, in small groups, will be given four slang words/phrases from the CW. Using the Internet, SW look up CW words and meanings using an assigned web site. **2.4** SW use chart paper to list their words and on an illustration from the Piece O' Pizza activity; SW complete 4 slices of the pizza.	**2.1** TW record students' answers on chart paper; encourage some phrases in students' L1; is there a comparable phrase in English? **2.2** SW download slang words and their meanings using the internet. **2.3** First 4 slices completed.
3. SWBAT compare/contrast CW slang and current slang and their meanings.	**3.1** SW brainstorm if their words are used in a present context; if so, they include an illustration on the other 4 Piece O' Pizza slices; if not, they select a current term or phrase that is similar.	**3.1** Completed Pizza/ identifying appropriate contexts, both historical and present; explanations of how current and CW are alike and different.
Language Objectives: **1.** SWBAT read and write CW slang words and phrases.	**1.1** SW present pizzas to the class describing the historical context using past tense verbs and present using present tense verbs.	**1.1** Students use appropriate tenses, past and present, to present their pizza. **1.1** Students' use of Civil War slang in context.

Wrap-up:
Tickets Out: SW write on slip of paper answers to the following:

1. Something I found really interesting . . . .
2. Something I wonder about . . . .

Source: Lesson plan created by Melissa Castillo and Nicole Teyechea. Lesson content created by MaryEllen Vogt.

FIGURE 9.2 *Secondary Lesson Plan for Review and Assessment*

Key: SW = Students will; TW = Teacher will; SWBAT = Students will be able to . . . ; HOTS = Higher Order Thinking Skills

SIOP Lesson: Civil War Slang Grade: *9–12*

Content Standard: NSS-USH.5–12.5 CIVIL WAR AND RECONSTRUCTION (1850–1877)

Key Vocabulary: Civil War, Battle of Gettysburg, slang, phrase, context **HOTS:** Why do you think the meaning of words and phrases used in the past have changed so much today? Do you think words and phrases we use today might change in the future? Why?	**Visuals/ Resources:** Computers and Internet access, Chart paper, markers; *Gettysburg: The Soldiers' Battle* story (or any literature book on the Civil War);

Connections to Prior Knowledge/ Building Background Information:

TW ask students to imagine that they are sent back in time to the Civil War (which they have previewed and will be studying): You meet a soldier after a battle and ask him about the war. Do you think you would have any trouble understanding his answer? Do you think people of that period used all the same words and phrases we do today?

SW respond to questions in their Social Studies Journals (10 min.).

SW share responses in an Inside/Outside Circle.

Content Objectives:	**Meaningful Activities:**	**Review/Assessment:**
1. SWBAT demonstrate knowledge of Civil War slang/key vocabulary by identifying words/phrases and their meanings.	**1.1** TW read the story aloud;	**1.1** Teacher observation and questioning during read-aloud
	1.2 TW emphasize slang words, for example: *chief cook and bottle washer; bread basket, graybacks, fit to be tied, hunkey dorey, greenhorn;* explain to students what is meant by *slang*. What are examples of slang phrases used today?	**1.2** TW record students' answers on chart paper; encourage some phrases in students' L1; is there a comparable phrase in English?
	1.3 TW ask students if they believe these words are still used today; if not what might be a word that means the same?	**1.3** SW download slangwords and their meanings using the internet.
	1.4 SW, in small groups, be given four slang vocabulary words from the Civil War. Using the internet, students will look up their words and meanings using an assigned web-site.	**1.4** First 4 slices completed
	1.5 SW use chart paper to list their words and the historical context in which they where used including an illustration from the Piece O' Pizza activity; SW complete 4 slices of the pizza.	**1.5** Completed Pizza/identifying appropriate contexts, both historical and present
	1.6 SW brainstorm how their words are used in present context by including an illustration on the other 4 Piece O' Pizza slices.	
Language Objectives:		
1. SWBAT demonstrate comprehension of Civil War slang/key terms vocabulary by orally describing historical contexts and changes in word meanings using past & present tense verbs.	**1.1** SW present pizzas to the class describing the historical context using past tense verbs and present using present tense verbs.	**1.1** Students use appropriate tenses, past and present, to present their pizza. **1.2** Students' use of Civil War slang in context

Wrap-up:

Is there a word that you use outside of school that means something different inside of school? Why is the context in which you use the word different?

Turn and share with a partner.

Source: Lesson plan created by Melissa Castillo and Nicole Teyechea. Lesson content created by Melissa Castillo and Kendra Moreno.

appendix a: the sheltered instruction observation protocol (SIOP®)

Observer(s): _____   Teacher: _____

Date: _____   School: _____

Grade: _____   Class/Topic: _____

ESL Level: _____   Lesson: Multi-day   Single-day   *(circle one)*

Total Points Possible: 120 (Subtract 4 points for each NA given: _____)

Total Points Earned: _____   Percentage Score: _____

Directions: *Circle the number that best reflects what you observe in a sheltered lesson. You may give a score from 0-4 (or NA on selected items). Cite under "Comments" specific examples of the behaviors observed.*

LESSON PREPARATION

4	3	2	1	0
1. **Content objectives** clearly defined for students		**Content objectives** for students implied		No clearly defined **content objectives** for students

Comments:

4	3	2	1	0
2. **Language objectives** clearly defined for students		**Language objectives** for students implied		No clearly defined **language objectives** for students

Comments:

4	3	2	1	0
3. **Content concepts** appropriate for age and educational background level of students		**Content concepts** somewhat appropriate for age and educational background level of students		**Content concepts** inappropriate for age and educational background level of students

Comments:

4	3	2	1	0
4. **Supplementary materials** used to a high degree, making the lesson clear and meaningful (e.g., computer programs, graphs, models, visuals)		Some use of **supplementary materials**		No use of **supplementary materials**

Comments:

(Echevarria, Vogt, & Short, 2000; 2004; 2008)

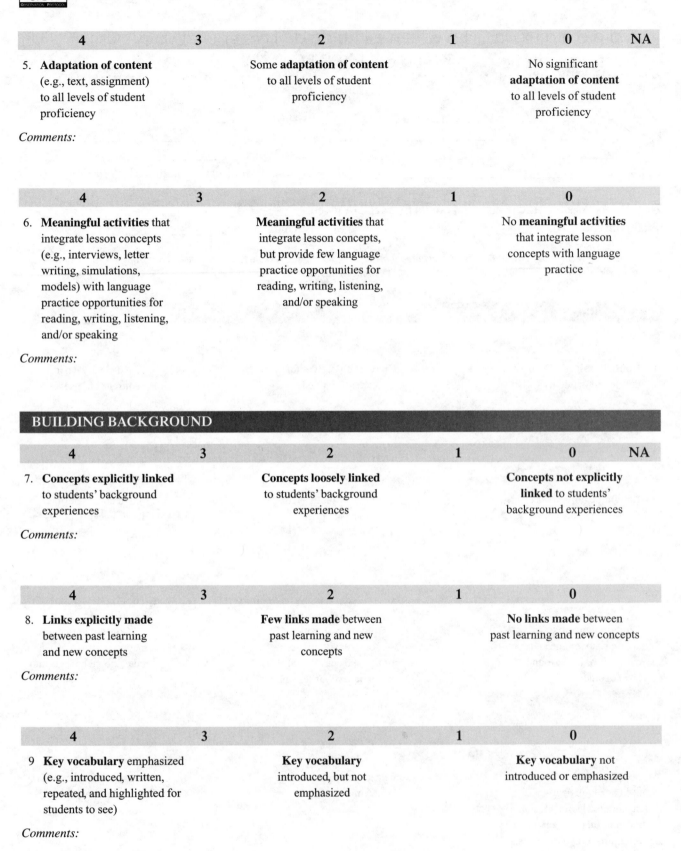

4	3	2	1	0	NA

5. **Adaptation of content** (e.g., text, assignment) to all levels of student proficiency

Some **adaptation of content** to all levels of student proficiency

No significant **adaptation of content** to all levels of student proficiency

Comments:

4	3	2	1	0

6. **Meaningful activities** that integrate lesson concepts (e.g., interviews, letter writing, simulations, models) with language practice opportunities for reading, writing, listening, and/or speaking

Meaningful activities that integrate lesson concepts, but provide few language practice opportunities for reading, writing, listening, and/or speaking

No **meaningful activities** that integrate lesson concepts with language practice

Comments:

BUILDING BACKGROUND

4	3	2	1	0	NA

7. **Concepts explicitly linked** to students' background experiences

Concepts loosely linked to students' background experiences

Concepts not explicitly linked to students' background experiences

Comments:

4	3	2	1	0

8. **Links explicitly made** between past learning and new concepts

Few links made between past learning and new concepts

No links made between past learning and new concepts

Comments:

4	3	2	1	0

9 **Key vocabulary** emphasized (e.g., introduced, written, repeated, and highlighted for students to see)

Key vocabulary introduced, but not emphasized

Key vocabulary not introduced or emphasized

Comments:

COMPREHENSIBLE INPUT

4	3	2	1	0

10. **Speech** appropriate for students' proficiency levels (e.g., slower rate, enunciation, and simple sentence structure for beginners)

                    Speech sometimes appropriate for students' proficiency levels

                                    Speech inappropriate for students' proficiency levels

Comments:

4	3	2	1	0

11. **Clear explanation** of academic tasks

                    Unclear explanation of academic tasks

                                    No explanation of academic tasks

Comments:

4	3	2	1	0

12. **A variety of techniques** used to make content concepts clear (e.g., modeling, visuals, hands-on activities, demonstrations, gestures, body language)

                    Some **techniques** used to make content concepts clear

                                    No **techniques** used to make content concepts clear

Comments:

STRATEGIES

4	3	2	1	0

13. Ample opportunities provided for students to use **learning strategies**

                    Inadequate opportunities provided for students to use **learning strategies**

                                    No opportunity provided for students to use **learning strategies**

Comments:

4	3	2	1	0

14. **Scaffolding techniques** consistently used, assisting and supporting student understanding (e.g., think-alouds)

                    Scaffolding techniques occasionally used

                                    Scaffolding techniques not used

Comments:

(continued)

4	3	2	1	0
15. A variety of **questions or tasks that promote higher-order thinking skills** (e.g., literal, analytical, and interpretive questions)		Infrequent **questions or tasks that promote higher-order thinking skills**		No **questions or tasks that promote higher-order thinking skills**

Comments:

INTERACTION

4	3	2	1	0
16. Frequent opportunities for **interaction** and discussion between teacher/student and among students, which encourage elaborated responses about lesson concepts		**Interaction** mostly teacher-dominated with some opportunities for students to talk about or question lesson concepts		**Interaction** teacher-dominated with no opportunities for students to discuss lesson concepts

Comments:

4	3	2	1	0
17. **Grouping configurations** support language and content objectives of the lesson		**Grouping configurations** unevenly support the language and content objectives		**Grouping configurations** do not support the language and content objectives

Comments:

4	3	2	1	0
18. Sufficient **wait time for student responses** consistently provided		Sufficient **wait time for student responses** occasionally provided		Sufficient **wait time for student responses** not provided

Comments:

4	3	2	1	0	NA
19. Ample opportunities for students to **clarify key concepts in L1** as needed with aide, peer, or L1 text		Some opportunities for students to **clarify key concepts in L1**		No opportunities for students to **clarify key concepts in L1**	

Comments:

PRACTICE/APPLICATION

4	3	2	1	0	NA
20. **Hands-on materials and/or manipulatives** provided for students to practice using new content knowledge		Few **hands-on materials and/or manipulatives** provided for students to practice using new content knowledge		No **hands-on materials and/or manipulatives** provided for students to practice using new content knowledge	

Comments:

4	3	2	1	0	NA
21. Activities provided for students to **apply content and language knowledge** in the classroom		Activities provided for students to **apply** either **content or language knowledge** in the classroom		No activities provided for students to **apply content and language knowledge** in the classroom	

Comments:

4	3	2	1	0
22. Activities integrate all **language skills** (i.e., reading, writing, listening, and speaking)		Activities integrate some **language skills**		Activities do not integrate **language skills**

Comments:

LESSON DELIVERY

4	3	2	1	0
23. **Content objectives** clearly supported by lesson delivery		**Content objectives** somewhat supported by lesson delivery		**Content objectives** not supported by lesson delivery

Comments:

4	3	2	1	0
24. **Language objectives** clearly supported by lesson delivery		**Language objectives** somewhat supported by lesson delivery		**Language objectives** not supported by lesson delivery

Comments:

4	3	2	1	0
25. **Students engaged** approximately 90% to 100% of the period		**Students engaged** approximately 70% of the period		**Students engaged** less than 50% of the period

Comments:

(continued)

4	3	2	1	0
26. **Pacing** of the lesson appropriate to students' ability levels		**Pacing** generally appropriate, but at times too fast or too slow		**Pacing** inappropriate to students' ability levels

Comments:

REVIEW/ASSESSMENT

4	3	2	1	0
27. Comprehensive **review of key vocabulary**		Uneven **review of key vocabulary**		No **review of key vocabulary**

Comments:

4	3	2	1	0
28. Comprehensive **review of key content concepts**		Uneven **review of key content concepts**		No **review of key content concepts**

Comments:

4	3	2	1	0
29. Regular **feedback** provided to students on their output (e.g., language, content, work)		Inconsistent **feedback** provided to students on their output		No **feedback** provided to students on their output

Comments:

4	3	2	1	0
30. **Assessment of student comprehension and learning** of all lesson objectives (e.g., spot checking, group response) throughout the lesson		**Assessment of student comprehension and learning** of some lesson objectives		No **assessment of student comprehension and learning** of lesson objectives

Comments:

selected references

Asher, J. J. (1982). The total physical response approach. In R.W. Blair (Ed.). *Innovative approaches to language teaching* (pp. 54-66) Rowley, MA: Newbury House.

Baumann, J., Jones, L., & Seifert-Kessell, N. (1993). Using think-alouds to enhance children's comprehension monitoring abilities. *The Reading Teacher, 47(3),* 184-193.

Bear, D., Templeton, S., Invernizzi, M., & Johnston, F. (2004). *Words their way: Word study for phonics, vocabulary, and spelling (3rd Ed.).* Upper Saddle River, NJ: Merrill/Prentice-Hall.

Dole, J., Duffy, G., Roehler, L., & Pearson, P. D. (1991). Moving from the old to the new: Research in reading comprehension instruction. *Review of Educational Research, 61,* 239-262.

Echevarria, J., Short, D., & Powers, K. (2006). School reform and standards-based education: An instructional model for English language learners. *Journal of Educational Research, 99*(4), 195-211.

Echevarria, J., Vogt, M. E., Short, D. (2008). *Making Content Comprehensible for English Learners: The SIOP® Model (3rd Ed.).* Boston: Allyn & Bacon.

Kagan, S. (1994). *Cooperative learning.* San Clemente, CA: Kagan Publishing.

Lipson, M., & Wixson, K. (2003). *Assessment and instruction of reading and writing difficulty: An interactive approach (4th Ed.).* Boston: Allyn & Bacon.

Macon, J., Buell, D., & Vogt, M. E. (1991). *Responses to literature: Grades K-8.* Newark, DE: International Reading Association.

National Reading Panel. (2000). *Teaching children to read: An evidence-based assessment of the scientific research literature on reading and its implications for reading instruction.* Washington, DC: National Institute of Child Health and Human Development, National Institutes of Health.

Ogle, D. (1986). K-W-L: A teaching model that develops active reading of expository text. *The Reading Teacher, 39,* 564-570.

Raphael, T.E. (1986). Teaching children Question-Answer Relationships, revisited. *The Reading Teacher, 39,* 516-522.

Readence, J. E., Bean, T. W., & Baldwin, R. S. (2004). *Content area literacy: An integrated approach (8th Ed.).* Dubuque, IA: Kendall/Hunt Publishing Company.

Say, A. (1993). *Grandfather's journey.* Boston: Houghton Mifflin Company.

Schultz, A. (1998). *Creative reading activities.* Workshop handout. Beach Cities Reading Association, Long Beach, CA.

Stauffer, R. (1969). *Teaching reading as a thinking process.* New York: Harper & Row.

Temple, C. (1998). *Reading and Writing for Critical Thinking Project.* Workshop handout. Tallinn, Estonia.

Vogt, M. E. (2000). Active learning in the content areas. In M. McLaughlin & M. E. Vogt (Eds.), *Creativity and innovation in content area teaching.* Norwood, MA: Christopher-Gordon Publishers.

photo credits